PROFESSIONAL ETHICS IN EDUCATION SERIES
Kenneth A. Strike, EDITOR

Justice AND Caring

The Search for Common Ground in Education

Edited by

Michael S. Katz
Nel Noddings and
Kenneth A. Strike

TEACHERS COLLEGE PRESS

Teachers College
Columbia University
New York and London

52.00

Published by Teachers College Press, 1234 Amsterdam Avenue, New York, NY 10027

Library of Congress Cataloging-in-Publication Data

Justice and caring : the search for common ground in education /
   edited by Michael S. Katz, Nel Noddings, and Kenneth A. Strike.
      p.   cm. — (Professional ethics in education series)
   Includes bibliographical references and index.
   ISBN 0-8077-3819-0 (cloth : alk. paper). — ISBN 0-8077-3818-2
(pbk. : alk. paper)
   1. Moral education—United States.   2. Educational equalization—
United States.   3. Social justice—United States.   4. Multicultural
education—United States.   5. Education—Aims and objectives—United
States.   I. Katz, Michael S.   II. Noddings, Nel.   III. Strike,
Kenneth A.   IV. Series.
LC311.J87   1999
370.11'4—dc21   98-35653

ISBN 0-8077-3818-2 (paper)
ISBN 0-8077-3819-0 (cloth)

Printed on acid-free paper
Manufactured in the United States of America

06 05 04 03 02 01 00 99   8 7 6 5 4 3 2 1

Contents

INTRODUCTION

Nel Noddings

Are care and justice mutually exclusive? Can one be subsumed under the other? Do they apply to different domains? What does each contribute to thinking about pedagogy and to policy-making?

In this volume, most of the chapters portray care and justice as moral orientations either in some tension with one another or working together to produce a more satisfactory solution than either could alone. No author takes the position that society can dispense with one or the other. Moreover, it does not seem that any author believes that care and justice belong to different domains. Most of us see the need for both, although it is not clear whether some of us would give one theoretical priority over the other. What has emerged for me in reading these chapters and reflecting on my own work is that care and justice may properly be applied to different moments or intervals in a moral episode or encounter. For example, justice-thinking may be necessary in stating a general policy on educational equity, but care is essential in refining and implementing it.

In my own chapter, I claim that justice untempered with care may actually introduce new inequities as it seeks to remove old ones. For example, when policy makers decide to eliminate the discrimination inherent in hierarchical tracking by forcing all students to take the courses once required only of students preparing for college, the talents and interests of many students are ignored, even denigrated. Several questions arise in exploring this situation: Is it possible to create a system of non-hierarchical tracks, any one of which could be chosen proudly by students? Might more minority students be included in college preparatory courses by adequate counseling and invitation rather than coercion?

Ken Strike argues for moral pluralism. He rejects both an ethic of justice and an ethic of care, because both suggest an exclusive moral orientation that denies what he sees as inevitable conflict between moral goods. Justice and care do not rule separate spheres, nor does one properly dominate the other. Rather, they sometimes work together to produce a genuinely moral solution and sometimes conflict with one another. Recognition of their complicity and conflict reflects accurately the moral complexity with which people live.

Dawn Schrader writes about the moral conflicts experienced by college students. She finds no clear-cut orientation (justice or care) in their thinking. Instead, concentrating on the process of working out moral problems, she claims that college students sometimes seem to draw on care-related themes, sometimes on justice. What shocked me—and may shock other readers—is the total lack of moral thinking evinced by some of the students she studied. Whereas Schrader generously speaks of "their moral psychology," I'd be inclined to speak of a psychology devoid of moral thinking. The examples provided should force us to think more deeply about how our society is raising and educating its children.

Michael Katz moves us directly into the realm of pedagogy. In a fascinating analysis of May Sarton's *The Small Room* (1961), Katz shows the conflict between care and justice as a young professor struggles to define her own role as a college teacher. In the case of plagiarism with which Lucy must deal, neither care nor justice can be fully satisfied. Moving toward care, Lucy grows and comes to see her role and academic life as far more complex than she had envisioned. Although hardly anyone could be entirely satisfied with the alternatives available to Lucy's college community, many of the participants learn something valuable about moral life as the story unfolds.

Both Ann Diller and Bill Blizek analyze the place of self-knowledge in moral life. Diller examines self-talk as an aspect of caring for self. If we heard another person talk as we do sometimes to ourselves, how might we (as carers) respond? Self-talk, as Diller describes it, can be facilitative and cautionary; it can steer us toward morally acceptable behavior. However, it can also be destructive and even reckless; in such negative modes, it can be careless of both self and other. Diller suggests that we need to learn how to listen to self-talk as we listen to the talk of others. In doing so, we may become more gentle and encouraging with ourselves, and less judgmental of others.

Blizek shows dramatically how our superficial understanding of care and justice may lead us to rationalize uncaring and unfair acts as moral ones. Wanting to be perceived as caring or just, we decide on acts that are motivated by neither. What we need to do, Blizek suggests, is to study ourselves more carefully as we think and talk about justice and care. The objective knowledge we hold about both needs to be complemented by self-knowledge so that our genuine motives can be brought into line with our behavior. Such reflection should nudge us upward toward more authentically caring and just lives.

When we turn to policy-making, we see again both the complementarity and conflict between care and justice. Rita Manning examines the issue of school vouchers from a variety of perspectives. She finds vouchers at odds with forms of liberalism that give a priority to distributive justice. Similarly, a voucher program is also in conflict with what she calls "connected communitarianism," a form of communitarianism that reaches beyond obligation to one's immediate community. Again, vouchers seem hard to justify from the perspective of a universal ethic of care. It may be possible, Manning concedes, to address the concerns she raises from each of the three perspectives, but the burden of proof is on those who advocate school vouchers.

Larry Blum explores the question whether multiculturalism is "divisive." He provides us with a typology of ethnicity and ways to categorize the values associated with ethnic communities and concludes that an examination of ethno-cultures yields a moral perspective that cannot be described entirely in terms of either justice or care. He would help us to steer a course between cultural chauvinism on one hand and a supposedly unified nationalism on the other.

Elizabeth Chamberlain and Barbara Houston look at sexual harassment policies in schools. Citing many empirical studies, they note that student-to-student harassment is common in schools. Further, it occurs with some frequency at just the point in schooling (grades 6–9) at which young people are called upon to make a commitment to serious study. Both academic and social identities are threatened by peer harassment. Taking a position similar to the one I adopted on equity, Chamberlain and Houston argue that both justice and care are required in the analysis of the problem, that justice properly guides the formulation of a policy, and that care is required in its implementation. In reading their chapter, I was reminded of a host of recent cases reported in the press involving "fair" policies gone mad in implementation—a child suspended for accidentally bringing a paring knife to school in her lunchbox, a six-year-old boy suspended for kissing a female classmate, children suspended for sharing non-prescription remedies with ailing classmates. If we add to these cases of lapsed common sense all those cases in which offenders fail to get the care they need to overcome their own insensitivity, we recognize a dramatic need for both care and justice. The educational objective, of course, should be not only to prevent harm and to ensure justice, but also to increase caring throughout the web of care so that offenders will be less likely to want to harm others.

To reiterate what I suggested at the beginning of this introduction, I think now that care and justice often apply to different moments in moral episodes. It is clearly not enough to make a just decision or to establish a just policy. One must follow up with caring implementation and with reflection guided by care to see whether the original policy has fulfilled its aims or has introduced new inequities or harms. And, of course, it may be, as both Blum and Strike suggest, that moral pluralism goes beyond care and justice.

PART I

Theory of Justice and Caring

CHAPTER 1

Care, Justice, and Equity

Nel Noddings

Debate on care and justice has often taken the form of strong opposition, care versus justice. It has also often concentrated on an alleged gender difference—women favoring care and men favoring justice. Although both debates are fascinating and include many questions that require better answers than we have now, they do not always attend to matters that should be of central interest to educators. To what degree should a concept of justice guide educational policy-making? What concept of justice should be used? Is justice (however we construe it) adequate as a moral orientation for educational planning? If not, can *caring* compensate for some of the inadequacies?

In this chapter, I want to show that justice, as it has been applied so far to issues of equity in educational planning, is clearly inadequate. I will then suggest how the care orientation might help us to think more deeply and clearly on these issues.

JUSTICE: CONTRIBUTIONS AND QUESTIONS

Justice has a long history. From the time of Socrates, Western philosophers have debated its meaning. At times it has referred to an inner state of serenity and well-being (the "just man" at peace with himself); at other times, it has connoted a desirable relationship with God; and in modern times, it has pointed more directly at a preferred relationship between institutions and human beings. Since the Enlightenment, the concept of justice has usually been tied to the notion of rights and impartiality. Within this contemporary framework, philosophers and political thinkers have disagreed about the origins or grounding for rights, some contending that rights are God given, others that they belong somehow naturally to human beings, and still others that they are products of reason. Among the last, further disputes have arisen over whether the rationality that produces rights is universal or conditioned by particular traditions (MacIntyre, 1988).

A central question for every modern theory of justice is who has a right to what. When John Stuart Mill (1859/1993) wrote about the right of "every" person to liberty—basically the right not to be restrained except from causing harm to others—he immediately qualified his remarks by saying that the doctrine of liberty as he had laid it out did not apply to children, other dependent young, and "barbarians." The doctrine was to be universal over a restricted class. Similarly, even today we argue over whether non-citizens should enjoy rights to medical care and education. In contrast, while some would restrict rights even within the human community, others argue for the extension of rights to nonhuman animals. Recently, debate over rights has become even more heated and complicated as some political thinkers criticize the 20th-century trend toward more and more individual rights. "What about responsibilities and social commitment?" these thinkers ask (Glendon, 1991). Still, other writers press us to think about granting rights to groups ("identity" groups) as well as to individuals (Galston, 1995). Several of these issues will be important in the following discussion of equity.

Despite disagreements over who shall have what rights and where rights come from, "rights talk" has given us a powerful language with which to demand universal justice and to criticize governments that abuse their neighbors or segments of their own populations. Campaigns for the civil rights of women and African Americans have been at the center of the drive for justice in the 20th-century United States, and the language of rights has also been used with considerable effect internationally. Thus, although I will discuss the need to move beyond frameworks of justice, it is clear that the emphasis on justice and rights has made an enormous contribution to human welfare (Dworkin, 1978).

In the United States today, the most widely discussed philosophical theory of justice is justice as fairness (Rawls, 1971, 1993). Besides its theoretical sophistication, it has strong roots in everyday intuition. At a very early age, children learn to shout, "That's not fair!" if they feel slighted or ill treated, and fairness has been the watchword in discussions of equity. The basic idea is that a society must establish rules that are fair to all and then live by those rules. Like related theories in the social contract tradition, Rawls's theory relies heavily on the notion of persons as rational and disinterested; at least, they must be capable of rationality and disinterest and willing to adopt this attitude at the start of their deliberations. In an "original position," where deliberants are ignorant of their own actual position in society, such rational people—it is contended—are likely to choose principles for their governance that will be fair to everyone. Rawls (1971) says that people starting with such a strategy will choose the following principles of justice for institutions:

> First Principle
>> Each person is to have an equal right to the most extensive total system of equal basic liberties compatible with a similar system of liberty for all.
> Second Principle
>> Social and economic inequalities are to be arranged so that they are both:
>> (a) to the greatest benefit of the least advantaged, consistent with the just savings principle [reasonable concern for future generations] and
>> (b) attached to offices and positions open to all under conditions of fair equality of opportunity. (p. 302)

We do not often find exactly this formal language in everyday discussions of justice, but the points of emphasis are familiar: people have *rights*; people are to be regarded as *individuals*; everyone should have a fair chance at securing desirable positions (*equal opportunity*); and if the rules cannot remove inequalities, they should at least be designed so that inequities favor the least advantaged. All of these are familiar (if controversial) notions in contemporary political conversation. As we will see, they are notoriously difficult to encode without a discussion of the goods people seek, and these goods cannot be limited to material welfare.

Before turning to a set of cases that will reveal the need for broader discussion, I should mention a competing concept of justice. The concept of justice as fairness is often referred to as a form of "distributive justice" because it concentrates on the fair distribution of a society's goods. Another concept emphasizes the just balance of goods and harms; "retributive justice," the most basic form of which is captured in the phrase "an eye for an eye, a tooth for a tooth," has a long history and is still dominant in criminal justice. Retributive justice necessarily involves the notion of *desert*. From this perspective, people do not simply "have" the rights so widely discussed in a given society. They must earn or deserve those rights, and even the right to life may justly be rescinded if one unjustly takes the life of another, betrays his or her country, or commits some other crime that the society has designated a capital crime. When the concept of desert is used in discussions of distributive justice, the debate becomes deeply complicated. For example, in establishing procedures for affirmative action (following Rawls's idea of favoring the least advantaged), the question arises whether we are justified in depriving one person of a position he or she seems to deserve on the basis of merit so that someone from an underrepresented group (also qualified) may advance.

Many more examples could be given of the clash between competing concepts of justice, but I want to show now that some important issues in educational policy-making require thinking beyond justice.

THE INADEQUACY OF JUSTICE

In 1954, the Supreme Court, in its celebrated *Brown v. Board of Education* case, used the Fourteenth Amendment to strike down legislation that established segregated education. The idea of "separate but equal" was demolished by the assertion that separate facilities are *inherently* unequal. Following the principle of justice that all citizens must enjoy equal protection of the law, it was judged clearly unjust to exclude black children from schools simply because of their race. Similarly, justice condemned the practice of forbidding black people the use of public restrooms, drinking fountains, theater seats, restaurants, or any other public facility.

But the claim that separate schools are *inherently* unequal requires deeper discussion. If it means that forced separation, separation without the consent of those directly affected, is necessarily unjust, then most of us would agree. Segregation by law, de jure segregation, is the form of segregation forbidden by the Court; it is this form that was branded inherently unequal. The injustice lies not only in whatever inequalities result, but even more deeply in the lack of consent of those concerned. Separation by law implies the inferiority or undesirablility of one group and thus has the potential to damage the self-esteem of those who are excluded from majority schools. Further, it is clear that the damage to self-esteem cannot be undone simply by providing "equal" facilities.

However, we need to ask why separation in and of itself is inherently unequal. Were the judges acknowledging that our society protects and sustains a dominant group and that placement apart from that group, even if one chooses it, inevitably creates a position of inequality? Were they suggesting that an all-black school in an all-black neighborhood is necessarily unequal to an all-white school in an all-white neighborhood?

The problem is enormously complicated. The court ruling was interpreted to mean that segregated schooling, however it occurs, is unequal. In practice, the solution decided upon was to transport children across neighborhood lines in order to achieve racial balance. In small districts, where neighborhoods are geographically close to one another, this policy often caused little hardship. But in huge city districts, where de facto segregation had created enormous enclaves of single-race neighborhoods, it became necessary to transport children over considerable distances. The defensible quest for justice thus ignored the possibility that neighborhoods would suffer a loss of community with the collapse of the neighborhood school. Alternative schemes to establish equality of material resources for neighborhood schools could not be tried (given the claim of *inherent* inequality), but if they had been, they would have run into the hard problem of school finance. If all-black schools were to be maintained, how could they possibly have equal facilities, given the poverty of so many of the districts comprising largely black neighborhoods and the widespread practice of raising school money through local (district) taxes? School desegregation through busing seemed the only answer.

However, there is another slant on the claim that separate schools are inherently unequal. There is the thinly veiled suggestion that black children cannot learn well unless they are schooled with white children. Even if evidence were to show that the achievement levels of blacks rise in integrated settings, other issues—possibly aggravated feelings of inferiority, more frequent experience of racism, and loss of community—have to be considered. At present, researchers still argue over whether desegregation has or has not produced improvement in minority achievement scores.

In a recent article, Kevin G. Welner and Jeannie Oakes (1996) argue for the benefits of both desegregation and detracking. However, most of the studies they cite on the effects of desegregation are both old and ambiguous. For example, with respect to achievement, M. Weinberg (1977) argued that the evidence was positive; E. G. Epps (1977) that it was inclusive; and J. S. Coleman et al. (1966) that there was no evidence of improvement. At about the same time, Derrick Bell (1977) argued along the lines I'm suggesting here that racism cannot be eliminated simply by desegregating schools. Rather, he contended, black parents and educators should be free to establish goals and design strategies for the education of their own children. Coleman's later work (1990) suggested much the same strategy. It is important to recognize that these advocates of choice do not deny the injustice of de jure segregation. They are worried about a form of harm that arises in addressing that injustice.

In a more recent study, Amy Stuart Wells and Robert L. Crain (1994) concluded that black students in integrated schools have higher occupational and educational aspirations than similar students in segregated schools. Of course, even if this conclusion holds, we do not know what effects might be found in situations where parents and students have genuine choice whether to attend a desegregated school or an all-black school.

Other studies (Dempsey & Noblit, 1996; Walker, 1993, 1996) have shown that the sense of community is badly disrupted when traditional "good" black schools are closed.

What I have said so far should not be interpreted as an argument against desegregation. It is meant as a call for thinking that goes beyond the usual pattern of justice-thinking. I have already agreed that de jure segregation is unjust; it is also uncaring. Further, it is clearly unjust to house black children in unsafe and unattractive buildings, deprive them of resources available to white children, and crush their spirit with poor teaching (Kozol, 1991). But the justice orientation often prescribes formulaic remedies and then pronounces the problem theoretically solved—remaining inequities are charged to faulty implementation—and, too often, it seeks an outcome, higher achievement, that it cannot produce. Care hesitates to make decrees; it would prefer cooperative decisions, a variety of desirable outcomes, and multiple options to achieve them. However, there are times when a just government must prod action through law. Probably no one embracing the care orientation would deny this, but we would point out that care often "picks up" where justice leaves off (Noddings, 1984, 1989). We do not suppose that ethical responsibility is finished when a just decision has been reached. Indeed, it is especially at this point that we must ask: What happens now to relationships? What happens to communities? What happens to the quality of experience for those who will undergo the consequences of our decision? If this kind of thinking were part of the original planning, justice might well culminate in broader recommendations. Thus, while caring often springs into action when justice has made a decision, it can also be used to anticipate likely consequences before a decision is made.

In the case under consideration, forced segregation would have been outlawed, but de facto segregation might have been regarded as more a symptom than a cause of inequality. Insisting that all children be cared for, not simply shifted about, would have opened the way for discussion of alternatives. In such a discussion, participants would have to describe the *goods* that they hold in common and those on which they may differ. It is not possible to care adequately for people without responding to their needs and interests. Universal rights, handed to people whether or not they seek them, cannot compensate for losses of identity, group respect, and community feeling.

Let's consider another example. Many educators and policymakers today suggest that all children should have exactly the same curriculum and that national standards and a national curriculum would work toward removing glaring inequities in public education. This debate, like most others we might consider, does not break out clearly along justice/caring lines. People can and do argue strongly from within the justice orientation for or against a universal curriculum. On one hand, it is argued that a form of equity might be achieved by holding all schools, teachers, and students to the same standard. Thus, it is said, the academic capacity of poor children would no longer be discounted at the outset. On the other, it is argued as strongly by other justice advocates that nothing could be as unjust as an attempt to achieve equity through sameness.

Mortimer J. Adler (1982) engendered a lively debate by reviving John Dewey's (1902) comment: "What the best and wisest parent wants for his own child, that must the community want for all its children. Any other ideal for our schools is narrow and unlovely; acted upon, it destroys our democracy" (p. 3). A superficial reading suggests the first solution—the same "top-notch" education for all children (Adler, 1982). But anyone fully acquainted with Dewey's work would know that Dewey wanted an education for each child that would match that child's interests and capacities. An advocate of justice, using the deeper interpretation of Dewey's words, would seek an equity that took account of differences.

Can a similar ambivalence arise in the care orientation? It certainly can if we use the words "care" or "caring" in everyday ways. People do all sorts of things in the name of caring. However, if we use *caring* as it is defined in current care theory, contradictory decisions—although still possible—are less likely to be made. *Caring* now refers properly to the relation, not just to an agent who "cares," and we must consider the response of the cared-for. As we respond to the needs and interests of individual children, we may see the need to design multiple curricula and to guide children carefully through the maze of possibilities. We prefer not to install universal policies that require coercion, because coercion produces resistance and weakens the relation. Treated like faceless cases, students often complain that they are not cared for, and as long as that claim is made, the relation cannot be said to be one of caring. But it is possible that a care theorist would argue for a standard curriculum for all children, insisting that children could be persuaded to accept this arrangement as a genuine expression of adult care—much as they accept compulsory education in general. However, notice that under either decision care theorists would have to argue for a vigorous program of dialogue and persuasion. Neither decision in and of itself could be properly called "caring." Neither a standard curriculum nor one sensitive to individual differences can be judged conclusively as caring. Children need more than a "caring" decision; they need the continuing attention of adults who will listen, invite, guide, and support them.

I think care theory favors a differentiated curriculum because it seems likely that as we work closely with students, we will be moved by their clearly different needs and interests. In any case, our claim to care must be based not on a one-time, virtuous decision, but rather on continuing evidence that caring relations are maintained.

To reinforce my point, consider the following. Suppose you are told that, since New York City students have been forced to take Regent-level mathematics, twice as many students have passed the relevant Regents' test. It is true, our informant admits, that failures have also multiplied alarmingly, but at least all youngsters now have a chance to do what only the relatively privileged did in the past. From one perspective within justice, advocates would point to what looks like equality of opportunity, and the number of passing students would be offered as proof that the strategy has worked. From another perspective within justice, advocates would want to know what happens to all the students who fail. Will they receive additional instruction and be urged to try again? Or will they be forced into lower status courses?

From the care perspective, the great increase in passing scores suggests that with appropriate guidance and enthusiastic invitation, many more children would successfully complete standard academic requirements without the coercion that dooms so many others to failure. But we would want to press the questions: Why *should* they? How do they feel about such studies? What would they really like to do in life? What special talents do they have that we should encourage? Looking at the youngsters who fail, we would be less concerned with whether they get a "fair chance" at another try than with the implication (and *fact* in today's education system) that any other course of study is necessarily of lower status. Do students who choose a vocational course of study thereby deserve a poorer curriculum and less considerate teaching? Must their course work prepare them less well for adult life? Our concern is to care for all our children and to respect all forms of honest work. Of course, children who want to try again on the Regents (or any other test) should be given help to succeed. But children who want to engage in occupations that do not require college studies should be given the opportunity to prepare for such jobs without any loss of attention, status, or care.

Education is not just preparation for economic life and citizenship. It is, as Dewey insisted, life itself. But even as preparation, it encompasses far more than getting a well-paid job. Ideally, it is preparation for caring—for family life, child-raising, neighborliness, aesthetic appreciation, moral sensitivity, environmental wisdom, religious or spiritual intelligence, and a host of other aspects of a full life.

Again, it seems clear that some advocates of justice could argue along roughly the same lines. The split is not a party-like division. The point is that care-talk enriches the initially narrow insights of justice. Justice draws to our attention the unfairness of a situation in which large numbers of children are deprived of the potential material benefits of schooling. Care cautions us to look at individual children before we recommend a remedy and to listen to those whose aspirations, interests, talents, and legitimate values may differ from our own.

I want to consider one more example before moving to the closing argument on equity. Some years ago, when I was a high school mathematics teacher, I decided to let students retake math tests as often as they wanted to within the time period allowed by district grading policy. My decision was based on long experience with students' test anxiety and the firm conviction that eventual learning, not a vigorous sorting-out, was the goal. If learning is our goal, I reasoned, why cut it off with a failing grade? When I announced this plan, one student immediately objected, "That's not fair!" He had received a grade of 92 (out of a possible 100) on the test that had triggered the decision and was outraged at the possibility that someone who had failed on the first try might get a 95 on the second. At least there should be a penalty, he insisted; surely, a 90 on a second try isn't as good as a 90 on the first try.

Once again, the justice orientation yields more than one perspective. One using a Rawls-like perspective might agree enthusiastically that my plan is entirely acceptable because it favors the least advantaged. However, another group might raise the question of *desert* that we discussed briefly earlier. People taking this perspective might argue that some students *deserve* another chance, but the careless and lazy do not; it is their own fault that they failed. Further, proponents of desert might suggest, a plan like this one might actually *encourage* laziness and negligence. Some students might take little care in preparing for a test, knowing that if luck didn't get them through the first time, they could always try again.

The care orientation doesn't produce this split judgment. One using it is as deeply concerned about the "undeserving" students as the deserving. Precisely because we want students to learn self-responsibility as well as mathematics, we will talk to them about their attitude and behavior. Luck might get you through, we admit, if you're smart and you've paid some attention. But for the most part, you will have to take responsibility for the results you want. What sort of *person* do you want to be? We are also concerned about the significant number of students who use failure as a cop-out. These students accept failure on a given test as an excuse to brush the material aside and hope for the best on the next unit. In mathematics, this is often disastrous, and the caring teacher will try to prevent it by urging (and perhaps even insisting on) a retest. Sometimes caring does suggest coercion! But the apparent need for coercion always signals that caring has not been completed in the cared-for. The teacher is exercising care as a virtue, but the relation itself is not one of caring, and a wise teacher will try to move from coercion to genuine persuasion.

I stuck to my new policy. Rather like the father of the Prodigal Son, I rejoiced with my students when they achieved a 90 whether that achievement came on the first try or the fifth.

CARE AND EQUITY

The three examples discussed above show that the split between justice and care is not clear cut, that divisions within the justice camp can be great, and that care-talk enriches the arguments offered by advocates of justice. When a just decision has been reached, there is still much ethical work to be done. I emphasized that fact here by noting that "care picks up where justice leaves off." Further, care-talk at the stage of deliberations may well broaden debate so that just decisions are appropriately informed by discussion of the goods and values sought by those affected.

In the theory I am defending, care as a moral orientation requires receptivity, motivational displacement (the direction of a carer's energy toward the projects or needs of the cared-for), and completion in the cared-for. Any policy that systematically precludes such interaction is ipso facto contrary to caring. Thus desegregation as the *only* lawful way to achieve racial equality, a uniform and universally required curriculum as *the* way to achieve academic equity, and classroom rules that proclaim their fairness on the grounds of impartial enforcement are all highly suspect from the perspective of care. Do the cared-fors *feel* cared for under these policies? Are their legitimate goods considered? Are relations of care enhanced or weakened?

Social policy guided by caring would try to establish conditions in which caring can flourish. Under such a policy, all the agencies of society would be brought to bear on the problem of inequality in education. Government would not try to "care" directly by imposing an arbitrary solution. Instead, it would provide the necessary resources for various groups to try reasonable alternatives.

Excluding any child from any school on the basis of race alone would be forbidden by both care and justice advocates. Justice theorists would argue for this rule on the basis of fairness. Care theorists, not disagreeing, would argue in addition that it is wrong to cause the pain and humiliation that accompanies such rejection. I should acknowledge here that the Supreme Court, in its justice-oriented 1954 decision, did note the damage to self-esteem inflicted by de jure segregation. John Rawls, in his theory of justice, also recognizes self-esteem as a universal good to be maintained.

But if the concern for self-esteem is really central to the orientation, it should carry over into a consideration of the remedy. What may happen to the self-esteem of children under the policies suggested as solutions?

Although I agree that de jure segregation is both unjust and uncaring, I would *not* argue that schools primarily intended for black children, or girls, or boys, could not be organized around the special needs of one group, but only that such schools could not exclude a "different" child who wanted to attend and understood the nature of the school's emphasis. If someone wanted to argue for exclusion (by rule rather than choice), he or she would have to show that the present network of care would be destroyed or severely disrupted by the presence of this "different" student. It would not be sufficient to argue that there is an "equal" facility down the street. Thus care advocates might well argue in favor of schools organized primarily for the betterment of some legitimate group, but they could not allow these schools to exclude students who want to attend and who accept the educational philosophy of the school in question.

The test of legitimacy for a given practice would always reside in the adequacy of conditions to respond to the needs of those for whom the practice exists. Suppose a school district announces that some of its high school mathematics classes will be designed primarily for girls. Boys will not be excluded from such classes, but they must understand that the selection of content and pedagogy will be done on the basis of what we now believe about women's psychology and political concerns. Will many boys insist on joining such classes? (Probably more would shout, "Unfair!" and insist on their "right" to participate if they were excluded than if they had to make a positive choice to join.) Are there any grounds for exclusion from the care perspective? I think there are, but the burden of proof would be on those who argue for exclusion. They would have to show that inclusion has made it demonstrably more difficult to care appropriately for the legitimately targeted students.

In some cases, the care argument might indeed counsel against inclusion. For example, the inclusion of some special-needs students in regular classrooms can be shown to make it very difficult for teachers to attend adequately to their main teaching duties. Neither the special-needs child nor the other youngsters receive the care they need. Some advocates of equity as sameness argue that "all children have gifts" and that the normally abled need to learn from special-needs children and vice versa. A care theorist can agree with this and still demur on mainstreaming that fails the test of providing adequate conditions for caring. Teachers and parents might, for example, organize part of the day (or week) around activities in which both groups can participate with mutual profit. In approaching policy-making in this way, we keep conversation and political action alive. We want policies that make it possible for local judgment to be applied and for institutions to address legitimate concerns as they arise. We do not establish one sweeping policy that is supposed to cover everything and then contrive arguments to rationalize decisions that are obviously faulty.

The same kind of argument can be used to allow the exclusion of disruptive students. Again, any principle chosen has to allow practices that make it possible to care adequately for both the disruptive student and the students who are receptive to learning (or at least to behavior that will not disrupt the learning of others). On one hand, suspension or expulsion rarely helps to establish relations of care for the offender. On the other, permitting disruption to continue or managing disruption with techniques that exhaust the teacher and deprive other students of opportunities both fail the test of care.

A skeptical care theorist might be forgiven for suspecting that many arguments for equity as sameness are thinly veiled attempts to achieve various economies. After all, it may indeed be less expensive to treat everyone alike than to give to each what each one needs. But even this goal (economy) is frustrated. Busing students to accomplish desegregation is expensive in both time and actual dollars, and the basic problems of unemployment and rotting buildings in inner cities remain untouched. Requiring the same curriculum of everyone creates the conditions for massive failure (and the need for potentially expensive remediation), for disruption caused by boredom and feelings of inadequacy (and, again, the need for costly remedies), and for the continued domination of values characteristic of a privileged class (thus setting the stage for ultimately expensive social unrest).

Besides the understandable desire for economy, systematic solutions are often driven by the encompassing liberal tradition that produced the theory of justice currently so popular. It is a tradition that has put great faith in progress, especially progress through scientific processes applied to social problems. Starting with the ideals we hold for ourselves, we are motivated to establish policies that will make these ideals accessible to everyone. We forget to ask what the people affected by such policies really want. The well-intentioned arrogance that marked colonialism still lurks behind many of our domestic policies (Colclough & Manor, 1991; Escobar, 1994).

I used "we" in the above paragraph because I include myself among those belonging to the liberal tradition. It may well be that we will have to move beyond liberalism. However, until we develop a way to do this without losing some of liberalism's great strengths, we should at least be aware of its weaknesses.

The care perspective does not entirely reject liberalism as an approach to social problems (Held, 1993; Tronto, 1993). But instead of assuming a false universalism, it recognizes deep and perhaps irremovable differences— differences which counsel against sweeping solutions that affect people's lives directly and preclude their effective use of self-chosen strategies. Care theorists usually seek ends compatible with justice, but we try to achieve them by establishing conditions in which caring itself can flourish. Out of this healthy environment of personal and community caring, solutions may emerge that will satisfy not only the criteria of justice but also the *people* who are the targets of our good intentions. What better path to equity?

REFERENCES

Adler, Mortimer J. (1982). *The paideia proposal*. New York: Macmillan.
Bell, Derrick. (1977). Waiting on the promise of *Brown*. In Betsy Levin & Willis D. Hawley (Eds.), *The courts, social science, and school desegregation* (pp. 341–373). New Brunswick, NJ: Transaction Books.
Colclough, Christopher, & Manor, James (Eds.). (1991). *States or markets? Neoliberalism and the development policy debate*. Oxford: Clarendon.
Coleman, J. S., Campbell, E. Q., Hobson, C., McPartland, J., Mood, A., Weinfeld, F., & York, R. (1966). *Equality of educational opportunity*. Washington, DC: U.S. Government Printing Office.
Coleman, J. S. (1990). Choice, community, and future schools. In W. H. Clune & G. Witte (Eds.), *Choice and control in American education* (vol. 1, pp. ix–xxii). New York: Falmer Press.
Dempsey, Van, & Noblit, George. (1996). Caring and continuity. In Deborah Eaker-Rich & Jane Van Galen (Eds.), *Caring in an unjust world* (pp. 113–128). Albany: State University of New York Press.
Dewey, John. (1902). *The school and society*. Chicago: University of Chicago Press.
Dworkin, Ronald M. (1978). *Taking rights seriously*. London: Duckworth.
Epps, E. G. (1977). Impact of school desegregation on aspirations, self-concepts, and other aspects of personality. In Betsy Levin & Willis D. Hawley (Eds.), *The courts, social science, and school desegregation* (pp. 300–313). New Brunswick, NJ: Transaction Books.
Escobar, Arturo. (1994). *Encountering development: The making and unmaking of the third world*. Princeton: Princeton University Press.
Galston, William. (1995). Two concepts of liberalism. *Ethics, 105*(3), 516–534.
Glendon, Mary Ann. (1991). *Rights Talk*. New York: Free Press.
Held, Virginia. (1993). *Feminist morality*. Chicago: University of Chicago Press.
Kozol, Jonathan. (1991). *Savage inequalities*. New York: Crown.
MacIntyre, Alasdair. (1988). *Whose justice? Which rationality?* Notre Dame, IN: Notre Dame University Press.

Mill, John Stuart. (1859/1993). *On liberty* and *Utilitarianism*. New York: Bantam Books. (Original work published in 1859.)

Noddings, Nel. (1984). *Caring: A feminine approach to ethics and moral education.* Berkeley: University of California Press.

Noddings, Nel. (1989). *Women and evil.* Berkeley: University of California Press.

Rawls, John. (1971). *A theory of justice.* Cambridge, MA: Harvard University Press.

Rawls, John. (1993). *Political liberalism.* New York: Columbia University Press.

Tronto, Joan. (1993). *Moral boundaries: A political argument for an ethic of care.* New York: Routledge.

Walker, Emilie V. (1993). Caswell County Training School, 1933–1969: Relationships between community and school. *Harvard Educational Review, 63*(2), 161–182.

Walker, Emilie V. (1996). Interpersonal caring in the "good" segregated schooling of African-American Children. In Deborah Eaker-Rich & Jane Van Galen (Eds.), *Caring in an unjust world* (pp. 129–146). Albany: State University of New York Press.

Weinberg, M. (1977). The relationship between school desegregation and academic achievement: A review of the research. In Betsy Levin & Willis D. Hawley (Eds.), *The courts, social science, and school desegregation* (pp. 241–270).

Wells, Amy Stuart, & Crain, Robert L. (1994). Perpetuation theory and the long-term effects of school desegregation. *Review of Educational Research, 64,* 531–555.

Welner, Kevin G., & Oakes, Jeannie. (1996). (Li)Ability grouping: The new susceptibility of school tracking systems to legal challenges. *Harvard Educational Review, 66*(3), 451–470.

CHAPTER 2

Justice, Caring, and Universality: In Defense of Moral Pluralism

Kenneth A. Strike

Justice aims at a society and at personal relationships in which people are treated fairly, where they get what they are due, in which they are respected as equals, and where mutually agreeable conditions of cooperation are respected. Caring aims at a society and at personal relationships in which nurturance and relationships are highly valued. When I say below that justice and caring aim at different *moral goods*, it is such differences as these to which I refer.

Because justice and caring aim at different moral goods, they may conflict. When teachers grade, they may wish to encourage, and they may wish to give each student what he or she deserves. They may not be able to do both. One account of such conflict is moral pluralism. Moral pluralism says that moral goods are irreducibly many and often conflict. It is part of the human condition that we cannot achieve every good fully in every situation. Moreover, there is no grand theory in which all moral goods are synthesized, weighted, and ordered.

A second account says that justice and caring are deeply different stances toward the moral world. There is an *ethic of* justice and an *ethic of* caring. Their associated forms of reasoning have different structures. They may be inherently at odds. Someone who thinks this may try to argue that one stance is superior to the other, to find a way to subordinate one to the other, or to achieve a synthesis of the two that resolves the conflict.

One argument that justice and caring are deeply different claims that justice is overly universalizing. Justice insists on general rules. It has a concept of the self that reduces everyone to a thin moral sameness and that denigrates the importance of particularities and relationships. Caring, in contrast, is context sensitive, has a situated self, and is fundamentally concerned for relationships.

In this paper, I focus on two arguments that claim to show that justice is too universalizing. I argue that the view that sees justice and caring as deeply different for these reasons is wrong and that an account of the tension between justice and caring rooted in moral pluralism is more defensible.

Consider some texts that illustrate the issues.

So act that the maxim of your will could always hold at the same time as a principle establishing universal law. (Kant, 1956, p. 30)

For the a priori thought of the possibility of giving universal law . . . is unconditionally commanded as a law without borrowing anything from experience or from any external will. (Kant, 1956, p. 31)

The steps for an actor in making any such a decision applying the Golden Rule based on ideal role taking are:

1.   To imagine oneself in each person's position . . .
2.   Then to imagine that the individual does not know which person he is in the situation . . .
3.   Then to act in accordance with these reversible claims in the situation.

This is clearly similar to Rawls's notion of choice under a veil of ignorance as to who in a moral situation one is to be. (Kohlberg, 1973, p. 643)

An ethic of care involves a rejection of universalizability, the notion that anything that is morally justifiable is necessarily something that anyone else in a similar situation is obligated to do. Universalizability suggests that who we are, to whom we belong, to whom we are related, and how we are situated should have nothing to do with our moral decision making. (Noddings, 1992, p. 21)

The moral problem arises from conflicting responsibilities rather than competing rights and requires for its resolution a mode of thinking that is contextual and narrative rather than formal and abstract. This conception of morality as concerned with the activity of care centers moral development around the understanding of responsibility and relationships, just as the conception of morality as fairness ties moral development to the understanding of rights and rules. (Gilligan, 1982, p. 19)

For Rawls and Kohlberg, as well, the autonomous self is disembedded and disembodied; moral philosophy is learning to recognize the claims of the other who is just like oneself; fairness is public justice; a public system of rights and duties is the best way to arbitrate conflict, to distribute rewards, and to establish claims. The standpoint of the generalized other requires us to view each and every individual as a rational being entitled to the same rights and duties we would want to ascribe to ourselves. In assuming the standpoint, we abstract from the individuality and concrete identity of the other. (Benhabib, 1992, p. 157–158)

These passages illustrate the tension thought to exist between justice and caring. An ethic of care, it is said, emphasizes relationships, and contextual judgments, and has a situated self. An ethic of justice, in contrast, emphasizes duty, rule following, and universal moral judgments and has an unsituated self. They also suggest the following two connected aspects of universality:

1. *Universalizability*: If R is a reason for person P doing action A in circumstances C, then R is a reason for anyone else doing A in any case relevantly similar to C.
2. *The Desituated Self*: There are certain universal characteristics of human beings (freedom, rationality, and equality, perhaps) that constitute human beings as persons. Moreover, equal respect for persons so understood is the central moral value. Because we are equal as persons, we have the same rights and obligations.

These two claims may be viewed as important to an ethic of justice. Each is resisted by an ethic of caring. In what follows below, I take up each notion in turn.

UNIVERSALIZABILITY, CONTEXT SENSITIVITY, AND LEGAL REASONING

Some philosophers claim that all moral arguments have the property of universalizability. *Universalizability* says that good reasons can be generalized to all similar cases. Related to this is the moral aspiration of reciprocity. In moral argumentation whether or not an argument is a good argument should not depend on who makes it. The essence of reciprocity is that in moral argumentation, we need to give one another reasons which all could in principle accept, regardless of how we are affected by the actions warranted by these reasons. This duty to reciprocity, in turn, is often defended by claiming that it is a duty we owe to other people by virtue of their status as persons. Hence there is a path that connects universalizability, reciprocity, and the (allegedly) unsituated self.

Properly interpreted, the logical ideal of universalizability surely does characterize all good arguments. As I have characterized it, universalizability is a formal rule of reasoning, and it is not specifically about moral reasons. It says nothing more than that if we think something is a good reason in one case, consistency requires that it be a good reason in a similar case, unless there is a relevant difference between the cases. Universalizability, so understood, precludes no conceivable form of context sensitivity. *Anything* that can be viewed as a difference in who we are, who are ours, or how we are situated can be viewed as a relevant difference between cases. What is crucial to the difference between justice and caring is not universalizability. It is our view of what kinds of things count as relevant reasons and relevant differences. Justice and caring may have different answers to give here, but that is a difference in moral goods, not a difference that results in justice insisting on universalizability and caring rejecting it.

Consider a case rather like Kohlberg's infamous Heinz case. Someone is faced with a choice between allowing a loved one to die and stealing a drug that could save the loved one. What does universalizability require? We might claim that the universality of the maxim "Don't steal" precludes stealing the drug in all cases, even if a life is at stake. Or we might say that because the value of respect for persons is overriding, we ought always to be willing to steal if a life is at stake. However, neither of these responses follows from universalizability. Universalizability does not support any general prohibition against stealing or any general entitlement to steal to save a life. It requires consistency only in what we count as a good argument.

Perhaps the problem is that if *I* want to steal in order to save the life of *my* loved one, I do not care much about whether this is universalizable. I care that *my* loved one may die. Universalizability is not sensitive to how *I* am connected to *this person*. But this is not clear. What universalizability requires is that anyone who says, "Since my loved one will die if I do not steal the drug, I may do so?" also be willing to say, "If your loved one were dying, you would be similarly justified in stealing the drug." Here universality recognizes the connection between two people as a reason. It does not reject the caring justification. It universalizes it. It resists only the idea that I can steal for the sake of my loved ones, but you under similar circumstances cannot. Universalizability provides no reason either for stealing or for not stealing the drug. It insists only on consistency—that any reason for me to steal or not to steal the drug is also a reason for you if you are similarly situated.

Suppose someone were to say, "I know it is wrong to steal the drug, but I am going to do so anyhow, because the life of *my* loved one is at stake." One way to understand this is to read it as saying, "There are some non-moral goods (such as the life of my loved one) that outweigh the moral obligation not to steal." This way of speaking narrows the meaning of *moral*, but it is still universalizable. Universalizability requires only that if this is a good justification, it is also a good justification in those cases that are relevantly similar. It is, however, no longer a *moral* justification. Now it says that sometimes non-moral goods trump moral ones. Suppose, however, we say that the phrase "I know it is wrong of me to steal the drug, but I am going to do so anyhow, because the life of *my* loved one is at stake" is not a *justification* for stealing the drug at all. It reports my intent, motivated by my love, but I do not view it as justifying my action in any way. On this interpretation, the claim is not universalizable. But since, on this interpretation, the phrase does not claim to be a justification at all, it is hard to see why we should view this as an objection to universalizability. Universalizability, after all, claims to be a feature of moral justifications. (See Love, 1986.)

Moreover, while this last interpretation may be viewed as an expression of caring, it cannot be what is meant by the claim that universalizability is objectionable because it desituates, for this last interpretation strips caring of any status as an ethical justification for actions. But presumably, those who argue for an ethic of caring believe that caring does give us ethical reasons for acting, reasons that are sometimes different than those given by appeals to justice. Here I agree. But now what seems to have emerged is that the tension between caring and justice is not a disagreement about universalizability. It is a tension between different moral goods.

A different objection is that universalizability is vacuous. The difficulty is that universalizability requires us to know *in advance* what features of a given situation make it relevantly similar or relevantly different to other cases. But that is exactly what we cannot know. Each case is different. Each case has unique features that make it sui generis. Morally sensitive people can only respond to each case in all its uniqueness. This is not inconsistent with giving reasons for what one does. In each case one can say what it was about this particular case that justified the response, but there is no hope of knowing in advance that what is relevant in one case will be relevant elsewhere. So while we can say why we did what we did in the instant case, we can never usefully generalize from this case to others. If so, universalizability has no cash value.

The virtue of this view is that it warrants a close look at each case. It inhibits running over cases with arbitrary rules, something advocates of situated moral judgments have rightly emphasized. This argument, however, will not distinguish justice and caring. An ethic of caring contains a substantive view about what moral goods are central to the moral life and about what count as relevant reasons. It says, for example, that in grading we must consider relationships with students as important and considerations about relationships carry more weight than (let's say) providing an equal reward for equal work. That is a theory of what counts as a relevant reason. Thus caring does seem to know in advance that relationships are relevant features of situations.

Perhaps the difference is that an ethic of care does not tell us what counts as caring in any particular case. We must carefully consider particular needs or interests to decide what counts as caring. And surely this, too, is right. But it is also true, for example, of the claim that we should give an equal reward for equal work. That does not liberate us from considering each piece of work individually and of having a conception of what counts as good work that is suitably flexible and may appropriately differ, depending on context. Good work in philosophy is different than good work in carpentry. In both cases, caring and justice, we have a view of what counts as a relevant reason. In neither are we liberated from considering the concrete case and applying our view of what is relevant in the light of circumstances and context.

Nevertheless, there is something to be said for the idea that conceptions of justice are often translated into rules that, because they may carry the force of law, must be obeyed even if a more context sensitive judgment suggests we should do otherwise. In real practice, caring seems to allow a higher level of flexibility in judgment than does justice. Isn't that the point? Here, too, I think that there is something to the claim. But unless caring is opposed to the very idea of the rule of law (which I trust it is not), we cannot uncritically claim that promulgating rules is itself objectionable. Here we need to ask about the point of promulgating rules.

The rule of law requires that rules be stated in advance. Laws must be public and predictable in their application. We could not have a society in which the rule of law counted and in which judges were able to make rulings on the basis of whatever they found relevant after the fact. The rule of law also constrains the exercise of arbitrary power. Finally making laws public permits their discussion. We could not have a democratic society unless we stated laws as general rules. Features such as these limit the degree to which the law can be context sensitive. "The law is a blunt instrument." We may try to anticipate likely differences between cases, and we may provide places in the law where judgment can be exercised. However, in the first case we make the law complex, and in the second we diminish the law's predictability.

Consider the ɪʀꜱ code. Perhaps we might hope to receive an instruction booklet that said only, "Send us what you think is fair." Our return could be put on a very small postcard. But we are unlikely to be happy about this for long if the ɪʀꜱ has the power to contest our judgment, especially if we can be fined or jailed as a result. Then we will want a tax code. The more we labor to make it fair and context sensitive, the more we will make it complex.

Case law is especially interesting here. The Bill of Rights is far from self-interpreting. What does it mean to say that "Congress shall make no law effecting an establishment of religion?" Can we have school prayer? Can we have voluntary school prayer? What kind of school prayer is voluntary? Can students say grace? Can they say grace over a ᴘᴀ system?

Courts interpret the Bill of Rights through the analysis of cases. When they hand down a ruling, it will be accompanied by an argument that provides a set of reasons as to why the meaning of some constitutional doctrine should be this and not that. These rules will take into account the point of the law, its history, and the facts of the instant case. Schools may not sponsor prayer. That lacks a secular purpose. Students may have religious clubs on school grounds on the same terms by which they may use school facilities for other extracurricular activities. The reason is free speech. Is religion altogether banned from the curriculum? No. Schools may make secular use of sacred materials. Students may individually thank the Deity for their food (even if it comes from the school cafeteria) or seek divine intervention for grades. These are private acts.

In interpreting the law, courts are supposed to follow precedent. This is a variation on universalizability. Courts must apply the law in the same way in similar cases. But what makes a case a similar case? That is what legal argumentation is about. Case law focuses on arguments that a new set of facts is relevantly similar to or relevantly different from those facts to be found in relevant precedents. Students have free speech, but their free speech is constrained by the material and substantial disruption standard. What if some students react violently to the speech of other students? Does that mean that we may forbid the speech? No, that grants hecklers a veto. Then must we permit students to wear T-shirts with racially inflammatory content? No, schools are not obligated to provide a level of security beyond their capacity in order to protect speech.

These arguments illustrate the real workings of universalizability. What is a good reason in one case is a good reason in another *unless there is a relevant difference.* What counts as a relevant difference is argued appealing to experience, history, current understandings of the purposes constitutional rights are intended to serve, and the argument of prior cases. These argumentative resources give legal arguments structure, publicness, and predictability. We would not have a Constitution if every consideration was equally relevant and every result equally possible in each case. At the same time the process of argumentation exhibited in case law provides a degree of flexibility for the Constitution to accommodate to new facts and new circumstances. We are not blind in addressing new questions because we have a basis in history, experience, and prior law. When the process works, it is neither so situated as to eliminate unpredictability nor so unsituated as to apply rules in ways that are oblivious to important differences.

In almost all moral reasoning, we must strike a balance between predictability and flexibility. The kind of balance required may itself depend on context. In some contexts the importance of predictability may be so overriding as to warrant inflexibility. When rules are enforced by the police power of the state, especially where trust in public officials is weak, it is imperative that we know what is required. In other situations where intimacy, love, trust, and care are present, predictability may recede and flexibility emerge. Every parent of more than one child will have heard, "Why can't I do X, when my sibling can?" Here we want to be able to say, "Because you or your circumstances are importantly different," and no sane person wants to run a family like a court. When it is clear to our children that they are cared for, when trust is present, it becomes easier for us to gain this kind of flexibility. Rules become guidelines, rules of thumb, and often the more thumb and less rule the better. At the same time, predictability is important for a child's sense of security and for responsible discipline. Children cannot be given limits apart from some rules. Moreover, children who find their parents capricious are unlikely to feel cared for. Here, too, finding a balance between conflicting moral goods is what is important.

Some conclusions: First, universalizability does not preclude situated judgments. Indeed, it is a presupposition of situated judgments that are not arbitrary or capricious. Second, what will (sometimes) preclude highly situated judgments are the need for publicness, the need for predictability, the need to constrain arbitrary power, and the need for democratic deliberation. These are needs that may be more important in legal contexts than in more intimate or personal ones, but they may be important anywhere. Thus while it may be true that the law generates general rules and that this constrains its context sensitivity, it is also true that this is done for the sake of certain moral goods that are crucial to a society which respects the rule of law. Third, the claim that justice reasoning involves a kind of universality that precludes context sensitivity is inconsistent with the kind of justice reasoning characteristic of case law, and since this is the basis of constitutional interpretation, we should not view this as a trivial example. The tension between predictability and flexibility, between general rules and context sensitive judgments, is a tension between moral goods. It is not about the form of justice reasoning versus caring.

Even if these points are correct, they may miss something important about caring, justice, and law. Perhaps the essential point is that in a world where there was more caring, we would need less law, and we would have less need to be concerned about justice. Quite likely, in a world in which there was more caring, we would have need of less law. Undoubtedly we would have fewer criminal courts (although this claim could also be made on behalf of justice). However, it is not true that the law or the concern for justice exists primarily to remedy a deficit of caring. Sometimes we have law because we need to know to what we have collectively agreed. No amount of caring would eliminate the need for traffic regulations or tax codes. Sometimes we have law because we disagree. We have different worldviews. No amount of caring is likely to eliminate the need for a clear view of the separation of church and state.

Moreover, caring is a relationship that we have with particular people. If I care deeply for *my* family, *my* friends, *my* community, *my* group, or *my* students, I may, as a consequence, be more rather than less tempted to secure advantage for them over your family, your friends, your community, your group, or your students. If I am a morally conscientious person, I will want to know what the bounds are on preferring those who are mine to those who are not. Sometimes, caring for one's own may need to be constrained by justice. Educators who are also parents often face these tensions. I may disapprove of tracking, but I want *my* children in honors classes. I may think that parents should not be allowed to influence unduly who teaches their children, but I want the best teacher for *my* children. In such cases, we need a collective understanding of who gets what when. We may need it more if we care for our own.

And it may be that if relationships are to be durably caring, they must also be just. Thus caring and justice may connect and compete in a variety of ways.

The argument of this section has shown that the claim that justice and caring are deeply different because justice requires universalizability and caring is situated and context sensitive is not true. It has also shown that sometimes in order to secure certain moral goods such as those that are associated with the rule of law, we may need to balance context sensitivity against such goods as predictability. These arguments suggest that moral pluralism is a better account of the tension between justice and caring than is the idea that justice and caring are deeply different.

RAWLS AND DESITUATED PERSONS

Doesn't justice emphasize equal rights which people have because they are persons? Doesn't justice claim that those features that constitute personhood are morally relevant and that others (our identities, relationships, and histories) may be safely ignored? Isn't this a paradigm case of the complaint that justice reasoning is insensitive to who we are and who are ours and presupposes an unsituated self?

We need a reasonable picture of the point of talk about persons. Suppose one argues that a right to due process is to be justified by an appeal to respect for persons and that this is a right all persons have equally. What due process requires is that we justify decisions made about people on the basis of reasonable evidence and that we have plausible standards for how such evidence is collected. That people have such rights equally is indeed meant to exclude certain kinds of factors as relevant to judgments. Judges, for example, are expected not to give harsher sentences to those convicted in their courts because they are black or poor or Catholic. Judges are expected to recuse themselves if family members appear before their bench. But due process can be context sensitive in several ways. In our decision making we are required to notice the relevant evidence that pertains to a particular case. In criminal cases we may notice who is guilty and who is not, and we may take extenuating circumstances into account in sentencing. Nor does the idea of respect for persons prevent us from considering context in deciding what process is due. High-stakes decisions require a higher level of due process. We may also balance the process due against other interests.

Thus with respect to due process (as elsewhere), the cash value of the language of persons is to combat bias, prejudice, and privilege and thereby to secure the equal protection of the law. When we claim that people are entitled to equal rights by virtue of their status as persons, we are saying that people are not entitled to preference in society because they are white, male, or wealthy. These characteristics are not irrelevant to every moral judgment, but they are irrelevant to the possession of basic rights. In the words of John Locke, governments "are to govern by promulgated, established laws, not to be varied in particular cases, but to have one rule for rich and poor, for the favorite at court, and the country man at plow" (Locke, 1690/1963, p. 409). Even this claim is reasonably viewed as subject to consideration. Affirmative action will illustrate. May we take race or gender into consideration in hiring or admissions? If we are entitled to the equal protection of the law, the best answer to this might be that there is a strong presumption that we may not take race or gender into consideration, but this is a rebuttable presumption. We must discover an important and legitimate purpose that is served by considering race or gender, and we must show that we cannot serve this purpose unless we consider race or gender. (This is roughly the prevailing legal standard of strict scrutiny. See, for example, *Board of Regents v. Bakke*, 1978) When may we take race or gender into account? Some plausible answers are when we are remedying an injustice, when diversity serves the goals of the marketplace of ideas, or when race or gender are job related. The plausibility of these exceptions to the rule depends on arguments that in such cases the use of race or gender as a criterion serves a legitimate public purpose.

There is no claim implicit in this language of persons and equal rights that precludes us from noticing all there is to notice about people in our broader lives. We may attend to the gender of the person we marry. We may consider all of the unique characteristics of a given person in our personal relations with that person. We can show preference to those who share our faith when we are in church. Justice, the equal protection of the laws, due process—these notions that are often linked to the language of persons—do not exhaust the moral life. So far as the law is concerned, they are rooted in a history that has sought to remove bias and privilege from our political life, and they are not motivated by any claim that only personhood is relevant to all ethical judgments.

Consider a different kind of case. In many school situations, we are inclined to prevent individuals from making decisions that immediately affect the interests of those they love or care about. For example, we are reluctant to allow parents who are employed as teachers to be the teachers of their own children. Similarly we are disinclined to permit spouses to participate in personnel decisions about one another. We view these relationships as conflicts of interest and sources of bias in decision making. Aren't these just the kinds of desituated judgments to which justice reasoning leads? The impartiality required by justice require us to ignore who we are and who are ours.

This is not the conclusion to draw. It is true that teachers who, *occupying the role of teacher*, treat their own children better than others in their class behave unjustly. But the caveat "occupying the role of teacher" is important here. It is needed because it would be quite inappropriate to claim that these same teachers, when at home and occupying the role of parent, have the same obligations to other children that they have to their own. It seems that while justice may require impartiality, impartiality should not be construed as broadly eliminating those special responsibilities we have to those we love.

It seems, instead, that how we expect people to act toward others depends significantly on the role they occupy. Teachers may not prefer their own children to others. Parents should. The role of teacher requires one kind of response and the role of parent another. The legitimacy of each is recognized, and they are different. That is why it is difficult for the same person to occupy both roles simultaneously. And rules that seek to prevent this not only serve fairness and eliminate bias, they also liberate people from moral no-win situations in which they cannot simultaneously fulfill the obligations each of their roles requires.

This example provides an important clue about how we may understand talk about persons. On one hand, we may read it as metaphysical talk about the human essence that asserts that the characteristics human beings have as persons are the only ones that are morally significant. Or we may read person talk as a way of describing the characteristics of human beings that are most important in a certain kind of context or to a certain kind of role, the role of citizen. The latter way seems more reasonable. Moreover, if we read person talk in this way, we need not accept the conclusion that person talk (and thereby justice talk) involves a desituated self.

Often complaints about desituated selves are directed toward the views of John Rawls. (See Chapter 1, this volume, for a statement of his principles of justice.) Rawls argues that principles of justice should be viewed as though they were chosen by self-interested agents behind what he calls a "veil of ignorance" and in an "original position." People in the original position know some things, but not others, about themselves. They know they are free, equal, and rationally self-interested. However, they do not know their race, religion, gender, or social position. In fact they don't know anything that individuates them from anyone else. They seem paradigms of desituated selves. Rawls imagines such individuals bargaining about the rules of justice which serve to regulate what he calls the basic structure of society.

Rawls has developed his views in two major works, *Theory of Justice* (1971) and *Political Liberalism* (1993). I claim that the objection that Rawls has a desituated self is unfounded. It may be a plausible objection to what Rawls says in *Theory of Justice*. It is, however, inconsistent with much of what Rawls plainly says in *Political Liberalism*. Rawls (1993) says the following about the original position, the veil of ignorance, and the argument for his principles of justice. The original position, he claims, is a device of representation and a thought experiment (pp. 24–28). He denies that the original position is a historical event or a characterization of human nature. The people in the original position are not viewed as real people. The view of the self involved in the original position is political, not metaphysical. (That is, it concerns people in the role of citizen.) The point of the original position is to model and explore the implications of certain assumptions about human beings (that they are free, equal, and rational) that are central to the political culture of liberal democratic societies (pp. 29–35). In short, Rawls views the original position as a part of a thought experiment about the role of citizen, not as a set of claims about human nature.

The central feature of the political culture of liberal democracies that is modeled in the original position is that no view of justice that assumes that some people are inherently entitled to preferential treatment over others can be adequate (p. 79). Catholics are not entitled to better treatment than Protestants or Jews, white people are not entitled to better treatment than black people, men are not entitled to better treatment than women. If so, then no argument of the form "We Xs are inherently entitled to better treatment than you Ys" can be a good argument for principles of justice. It is the point of the original position and the veil of ignorance to prevent such arguments (by means of the fiction that people do not know what religion, race, gender, and so forth, they are) from being employed as arguments for basic principles of justice and to insist that people must argue for principles of justice from the starting points of political equality and freedom.

The original position does not characterize Rawls's overall view of moral argumentation or his overall view of the moral life. In fact, it is a relatively small part of it. For example, Rawls (1971) claims that people need to develop two moral powers (pp. 81–85). The first is the capacity for a sense of justice. The second is the capacity to form a conception of the good. In neither case is the kind of reasoning involved which was described in the original position. Rawls views the principles of justice achieved in the original position as means for selecting constitutional principles and these as the background principles that form a conception of public reasoning. However, the selection of constitutional principles and the appeal to such principles in public reasoning is not done in the original position or behind a veil of ignorance (pp. 212–254). People do know who they are and what their society is like. They are aware of their political traditions and the histories of their own society and may take these into account.

It is especially important to Rawls's project in *Political Liberalism* (1993) to insist that people are not viewed as desituated in the exercise of the second moral power. Rawls claims that citizens have a conception of the good that is exercised in the light of a comprehensive doctrine (p. 81). A religion is an example of a comprehensive doctrine. He characterizes a comprehensive doctrine as a tradition (p. 59). The forms of moral reasoning associated with comprehensive doctrines are embedded in history and in a community context. In those cases where Rawls talks about the relation of people to their society, selves with distinct identities are viewed as situated in and formed by a historical and cultural context. One example:

Rawls argues that leaving one's country involves leaving "the society and culture whose language we use in speech and thought to express and understand ourselves, our aims, goals, and values; the society and culture whose history, customs, and conventions we depend on to find our place in the world" (1993, p. 222).

Finally, and crucially, the distinction between ethical and political liberalism, one that is central to the project and argument of *Political Liberalism*, turns on the rejection of autonomy as a necessary personal ideal. It is autonomy that is central to the ideals of ethical liberalism, and it is the commitment to autonomy that brings ethical liberals into conflict with cultures that view their members as fully embedded in a tradition in such a way as to reject the view that everyone should have an unencumbered choice of his or her own good. It is the commitment to autonomy that has often led commentators to see a kind of featureless self, a rational chooser behind every choice, as central to Rawls's picture of the self (see Sandel, 1982, and for rebuttal, Larmore, 1987), and it is this picture of autonomy that Rawls rejects in *Political Liberalism*. Thus there is no desituated self in Rawls, not in his view of the relation of individuals to their culture, not in his view of autonomy, not in his characterization of the second moral power and the relation of people to traditions, and not in justice reasoning. The view that Rawls has a desituated self involves both a misunderstanding of the original position and an extrapolation of the reasoning in the original position to the whole of the moral life. Even if ascribing this view to him on the basis of his views in *A Theory of Justice* is plausible, it is difficult to reconcile the claim with *Political Liberalism*.

These comments about Rawls may be difficult to follow for those unfamiliar with his work. I have discussed them, because the criticism that Rawls has a desituated self is common in the literature and has been an important part of the argument that justice and caring are deeply different. The point of these arguments, however, is simple. In his discussion of the original position and the veil of ignorance, Rawls is not claiming that freedom, equality, and rationality constitute the essence of human nature or that they are all that are relevant to moral argumentation. He is doing two things. First, he is exploring the features of a role. He is not saying that who we are or who are ours never count. He is saying that in our role as citizen we cannot seek to rig the rules of justice so that they favor us and ours. The rational agents in the original position are like the teacher who cannot prefer his or her own students in the role of teacher, but who can in the role of parent. Second, Rawls is affirming the importance of what I earlier called reciprocity. If we are to engage other citizens in dialogue, we must be willing to give reasons that all can accept. But arguments that say, "I am entitled to better treatment than you because I am white, or male, or Protestant, or wealthy" are not arguments that all can accept. Hence Rawls attempts to understand the role of citizen through the fiction that since people do not know who they are, they cannot employ such arguments in reasoning about justice. But nothing in Rawls's view suggests that outside of the role of citizen, we are unable to consider the full range of characteristics that people have or that who we are and who are ours are, for all purposes, irrelevant. As a citizen, I may not claim that public schools should treat my children better than yours, but I may read to my children and not yours at home. As a citizen, I may not insist that the government prefer my church to yours, but I may contribute to my church and not yours. Rawls's device of the original position and the veil of ignorance may not be the best way to develop these points (see Strike, 1994), but they do not involve a desituated self. They seek fairness and impartiality in public life.

Let me recapitulate the argument to this point. The case that justice and caring are deeply different has been thought to depend on claims such as that universalizability and reciprocity decontextualize moral judgments and that appeals to personhood involve a desituated self in which who we are and who are ours counts for little morally. I have shown that these claims are largely untrue. The conclusion to draw, I believe, is that while justice and caring affirm different moral goods, they are not deeply different views of the moral life. The tensions between them are best understood from the perspective of moral pluralism.

CONCLUSIONS AND MORAL EDUCATION

There is more to the moral life than justice or caring. There is craft and civility and charity and commitment and awe and devotion and refinement and obedience and humility and honor and (especially, I think) kindness—and much else. We cannot deal with this array of moral conceptions by means of theories that reduce the moral life to a contest between justice and caring. Moral pluralism provides a more adequate view of moral complexity and moral conflict.

Three conclusions about moral education follow. The first is that we need to be very careful in our reflections on education that we not substitute part of the moral life for the whole. Merely to ask the question "Justice or caring?" as though when we had answered it we had encompassed the moral life is wrong.

Second, within the context of moral pluralism, the virtues of wisdom, judgment, and the capacity to strike a balance, to find the mean, are especially important. While justice and caring are not in tension in some deep way, they (along with other moral concepts) may come into tension in particular cases. To sort out such cases of moral ambiguity, children need to learn to see how moral conceptions are attached to the purposes they serve, else they will become mindlessly rule following. They need to be able to see situations in their complexity, else they will allow some purposes and moral conceptions to inappropriately rule over others. And they need to learn the art of striking a reasoned balance when purposes and moral conceptions compete. Finally, they need to understand that in the best of choices there is often something lost as well as something gained.

Third, the appreciation of moral complexity that moral pluralism affords may be an aid in promoting tolerance and reciprocity. Moral pluralists are likely to resist the use of simplistic dualisms to characterize (and dismiss) the views of others. If we recognize the complexity of the moral life, we are more likely also to recognize the struggles of others as they seek to find a balance in their lives, and we are more likely to view others as people, like ourselves, who are engaged in complex choices that do not have easy answers.

REFERENCES

Benhabib, Syla. (1992). *Situating the self: Gender, community and postmodernism in contemporary ethics*. New York: Routledge, Chapman & Hall.

Board of Regents v. Bakke, 98 S. Ct. 2733 (1978).

Fullinwider, Robert. (1995). Citizenship, individualism, and democratic politics. *Ethics, 105*(April), 497–515.

Gilligan, Carol. (1982). *In a different voice*. Cambridge: Harvard University Press.

Kant, Immanuel. (1956). *Critique of practical reason*. New York: Bobbs-Merrill.

Kohlberg, Lawrence. (1973). The claim to moral adequacy of a highest stage of moral judgment. *Journal of Psychology, 70*, 630–646.

Larmore, Charles. (1987). *Patterns of moral complexity*. Cambridge: Cambridge University Press.

Locke, John. (1963). *Two treatises of government*. New York: Cambridge University Press. (Original work published 1690.)

Love, Charles. (1986). Universalization, projects, and the new feminine ethic. *Philosophy of Education: 1986, Proceedings of the Forty-Second Annual Meeting of the Philosophy of Education Society*, pp. 73–82.

Noddings, Nel. (1992). *The challenge to care in schools: An alternative approach to education*. New York: Teachers College Press.

Rawls, John. (1971). *A theory of justice*. Cambridge, MA: Harvard University Press.

Rawls, John. (1993). *Political liberalism*. New York: Columbia University Press.

Sandel, Michael. (1982). *Liberalism and the limits of justice*. Cambridge, Cambridge University Press.

Strike, Kenneth. (1994). On the construction of public speech: Pluralism and public reason. *Educational Theory, 44*, 1: 1–25.

CHAPTER 3

Justice and Caring: Process In College Students' Moral Reasoning Development

Dawn E. Schrader

Students face complex dilemmas during their college years. Challenged perhaps for the first time by conflicting values, they seek to answer moral questions about justice and fairness, caring and responsibility. While college students' reasoning can and has been characterized according to the current moral theories of Lawrence Kohlberg and Carol Gilligan, something else is "going on" in their construction of meaning in their moral world. Boyd (1981) transformed our understanding of development toward postconventionality when he articulated the concept of "sophomoritis"—a form of moral relativism that occurs during the college years as students question their personal moral commitments and also the enterprise of doing so. College students are working hard to find the balance between themselves and others and society, struggling with considerations of both justice and caring while struggling to create a system of beliefs and behaviors which constitute a moral self and a moral life. This chapter briefly glimpses at this process. It is not so much about people's moral stage reasoning or justice and care orientations, nor is it about the final result of a reasoning process that results in moral or immoral outcomes. It is about the kinds of struggles and components that are used by college students as they struggle with the complexity of moral issues that they perceive in their daily lives. In short, it is a brief look at a living process of how some college students experience their moral realities.

Research in moral psychology and education tends to dichotomize justice and care. Questions posed in the literature include: Do people perceive dilemmas that involve predominantly justice or care concerns? Do they resolve those dilemmas using justice or care considerations? Can people "switch" orientations, depending on the context? Is the moral problem solver, the "self," autonomous or connected in its resolution strategy? Since the early 1980s, research in moral psychology sought to articulate differences between justice and care as orientations to moral decision making, to examine gender differences in their use (Attanucci, 1988; Brown, et al, 1988; Gilligan, 1977, 1982; Johnston, 1988; Lyons, 1983) and to articulate the nature of linkages, if any, between moral orientation and Kohlberg's stage theory (Gilligan, 1982; Colby & Kohlberg, 1987; Walker, de Vries, & Trevethan, 1987; Gibbs, Arnold & Burkhart, 1984).

The polarization of justice and care was established early in the research enterprise. First, Gilligan's use of real life situations contrasts starkly with Kohlberg's emphasis in his moral development theory on hypothetical situations, which establishes a natural opposition to the two theorists' work. Kohlberg's philosophical psychology of morality is concerned with prescriptive, universalizable judgments made under hypothetical circumstances by an impartial moral agent. Gilligan's psychological approach to morality is concerned with particularistic reasoning about real situations in which the self is inextricably linked. Another main polarizing issue involves assumptions about psychological development. Following Piagetian constructivist psychology, Kohlberg assumes that people's reasoning develops along a hierarchical sequence; that once a particular stage of moral reasoning or cognitive perspective is constructed, meaning is interpreted through that perspective until perturbance in that structure offers opportunities for reconstruction. Gilligan objects to this viewpoint, rejecting its male bias, hierarchical nature, and focus on universality.

The polarization stems primarily from the disjuncture between Kohlberg's theory as a philosophical hermeneutics, which he calls a "rational reconstruction of the ontogenesis of justice reasoning," and Gilligan's psychological hermeneutics, which is a type of literary analysis of the moral issues as narrated by individuals. Kohlberg and Gilligan thus have somewhat different conceptualizations of the justice domain, and Gilligan has offered a conceptualization of care as a different "voice" of morality that is used primarily by women. Gilligan (1982) writes:

> all human relationships, public and private, can be characterized *both* in terms of equality and in terms of attachment, and . . . both inequality and detachment constitute grounds for moral concern. Since everyone is vulnerable both to oppression and to abandonment, two moral visions—one of justice and

one of care—recur in human experience. Two moral injunctions, not to act unfairly toward others, and not to turn away from someone in need, capture these different concerns. (p. 20)

Thus it does not seem that justice and care are the issues that should be on opposite sides of a continuum. Rather, they should be seen together, and it is the philosophical and methodological issues that are at odds. Bill Puka (1991) examines these issues, and concludes that Kohlberg's vision of the development of moral reasoning and Gilligan's vision of care might be nurtured together. Walker, de Vries, and Trevethan (1987) empirically support this view in their study of 80 family triads. They find that (1) stage consistency was exhibited between real and hypothetical dilemmas, (2) few individuals used a single moral orientation, (3) no sex differences were observed for gender and stage, and (4) relationships between orientation and stage were inconsistent. In addition, Colby and Damon's (1992) moral exemplars integrate justice and care considerations when approaching moral dilemmas and issues in their daily lives. The authors claim that they do so regardless of their Kohlbergian moral stage; that is, they are not all postconventional reasoners. This chapter will demonstrate that one need not be morally exemplary or postconventional to have justice and care resonating together to form a blending of the voices and create a full sounding of moral issues in everyday life. Indeed, moral exemplars "do not form their self identities in a wholly different manner from other people" (Colby & Damon, 1992, p. 301). Thus we, as moral researchers and educators, must look at the *process* of how people begin to struggle to articulate their moral voice or voices on the way to constructing a moral meaning system.

The questions I ask as a moral psychologist and educator of college students are: What makes something moral? How do students think about moral issues? Are their thoughts different in hypothetical moral situations and in their daily lives? Do the dichotomous descriptions of moral psychology characterize their thinking? If the current trends investigating moral reasoning continue, one need only ascertain students' moral stage and moral orientation to understand their reasoning and actions. This approach is, of course, inadequate. College students' reasoning has moral complexity that isn't evidenced in much of the literature in the justice-care debate. And with the significant contribution of researchers such as Carol Gilligan (1982), Nona Lyons (1983), and Augusto Blasi (1990), the conceptualization of self in relation to morality adds dimension to the territory of gender and moral orientation.

As college students struggle with self-identity and moral reflection, their thought processes are a potentially fertile ground for observing how interrelationships between conceptualizations of care and justice are constructed. This chapter discusses the interrelationships I see between the theories of Kohlberg and Gilligan, reports the types of dilemmas students discuss and the cognitive strategies and resolutions used in resolving real life dilemmas, and then describes one case as an illustration of the struggle of moral meaning making. I conclude with some implications for research on moral theories and education.

RELATIONSHIPS BETWEEN JUSTICE AND CARE

Apart from our relationships with others, there is no moral necessity. (Piaget, 1932/1965, p. 196.)

Jean Piaget articulated several conceptualizations of the justice and care aspects of moral reasoning in his monograph *The Moral Judgment of the Child* (1932/1965). He defined morality in terms of justice and the development of a conceptualization of rules, and although he observed gender-based differences in the complexity of the understanding of rules, he concluded that girls and boys followed the same trajectory in the underlying structure of reasoning about moral issues. The differences Piaget observed included the type of "games" played, a different rule structure of those games, and a different form of resolutions to those disputes. Specifically, boys played marbles—a game involving complex rules—and when rule infractions were observed, boys tended to resolve those issues through debate and argument. Girls played a less complex and more social game—hopscotch—and when rule infractions occurred, girls resolved them though accommodation, inclusion, and/or changing the game, rather than by debating the rules. These issues continue to be observed in moral psychology: different "games" parallel the different types of dilemmas considered to be moral by males and females, and the differences in rule structure and resolutions seems to parallel the focus on justice and care.

Kohlberg and Gilligan have built on these early observations in some fashion. Kohlberg's roots in Piagetian theory are obvious. He accepted Piagetian notions of justice as morality, accepted the assumptions underlying cognitive structuralism, elaborated his stage sequence that requires specific Piagetian cognitive operations at each level of moral reasoning, and extended his moral theory beyond the structural qualities with his conceptualization of moral types A and B, which he calls heteronomy and autonomy. These are the same labels Piaget ascribes to the process of moral development of children, yet their application and use are seen throughout adult development (Tappan, Kohlberg, Schrader, & Higgins, 1987). Kohlberg's research enterprise was to elaborate the conceptualization of morality into the teenage and adult years. This enterprise resulted in Kohlberg's two main contributions to psychology: his stage developmental theory, with its corresponding interviewing technique and scoring system(s), and his moral education theory. Kohlberg's strict adherence to Piagetian characteristics of stage has been the target of much criticism over the years. And perhaps Kohlberg was more Piagetian than Piaget when one considers the nature of Piaget's later work on constructivism and possibility (Beilin, 1992). He assumes moral development occurs in an invariant, hierarchical stage sequence that is universal. Since research reflects the historical moment in which it is constructed, Kohlberg was constrained by the dominant paradigm of the time, which resulted in the construction and use of hypothetical dilemmas that focused interview respondents on two conflicting moral issues such as life versus law, morality and conscience versus punishment, or contract versus authority (Colby & Kohlberg, 1987). This was done both to focus on the underlying stage structure and avoid a structure-content confusion. The classic structure-content issue is seen in Gilligan's (1982) observation that women are disporportionately scored at stage 3 because they use care as a moral consideration. The newest coding manual clearly separates norms and elements within and between stages and redresses that concern (Colby & Kohlberg, 1987). Another examination into the structure-content issue was conducted by Gibbs, Arnold, & Burkhart (1984) in their analysis of the use of norms by stage. They found that while no stage differences existed, women tended to use affiliation more often in their considerations than did men. Despite additional inquiry since then (e.g., Baumrind, 1986; Walker, 1984, 1986), the gender differences question regarding stage and content is still debated.

Kohlberg contends that his moral conceptualization does not exclude care nor relegate it to stage 3. Kohlberg (1984) defends his theory and its underlying assumptions by demonstrating its cross-cultural and cross-gender applicability, and by showing how the content of the dilemmas elicits both justice and caring considerations (or norms). Specifically, even though the Heinz dilemma, for example, juxtaposes justice issues of life versus law in the interview at what he calls the "issues" level (that is, what action choice should Heinz take: steal and uphold human life, or not steal and obey the law), respondents frame the dilemma and use their own conception of the moral considerations to resolve the dilemma. Kohlberg uses the concepts of "norms" and "elements" in his scoring system to represent these considerations. Norms include such moral conceptions of affiliation, truth, conscience as well as the general action-choice issues mentioned above. In addition, Kohlberg's theory is construed primarily in terms of deontological elements. Some of these elements have been utilized in conceptualizations of moral orientations, specifically, the "normative order" orientation toward rulefulness or lawfulness and duty are seen as characterizing the justice orientation in Lyons's (1982) coding scheme and Brown et al.'s (1988) reading guide. But Kohlberg's inclusion of teleological ethics appears in two groups of elements: utilitarianism and perfectionism. Utilitarianism, as Kohlberg derived it from Bentham and Mill, includes considerations that "maximize the welfare or happiness consequences of all the individuals affected." Perfectionistic ethics is included in the elements that refer to "the movement toward harmony both within and among persons" (Colby & Kohlberg, 1987, p. 52). In sum, although the hypothetical dilemmas appear to bias Kohlberg's moral domain in terms of justice alone, Kohlberg contends:

> Although Gilligan (1982) has argued that because of the focus on justice as the central defining feature of the moral domain, the system fails to account for an important area of morality that she calls caring and responsibility. Although it is true that the dilemmas in the Standard Moral Judgment Interview pose conflicts of rights, the actual judgments made by respondents may focus on concern and love for another person, on personal commitments, on the need for sympathy and understanding, on responsibility to humanity and one's fellow human beings as well as rights, rules, and duties. As long as these concepts are used prescriptively, as defining what is morally right or good, they fall within the scope of the moral domain as we construe it. In this sense, the scope of the domain we assess is considerably broader than is conveyed by the term *justice reasoning*. (Colby & Kohlberg, 1987, p. 11)

Gilligan is likewise influenced by Piaget, Kohlberg, and the historical moment of engaging in the research enterprise, but she acted in reaction to it. She, like Piaget, saw that girls played a different moral "game"—but her observations were not like those that Piaget observed among girls who played hopscotch. Rather, Gilligan saw a bigger game in which women's voices are not heard and where men make the rules: real life. She observed that women construct their moral problems and decisions in terms of conflicting responsibilities and webs of relationships (Gilligan, 1977, 1982). Gilligan thus changed the moral "game." Her observations forever changed the approach to the study of morality from Piaget's and Kohlberg's search for how people develop their conceptualization of rules to how women define moral problems and make moral choices in real life situations. Justice considerations were heard in women's voices, but women use the care voice predominantly (e.g., Brown et al., 1988; Johnston, 1988). Unlike Kohlberg's justice focus, with all of its corollary cognitive constructions, Gilligan's care orientation includes considerations such as avoiding hurt as a moral problem, a web of interdependence, a concept of being there, listening as a moral act, understanding, shared responsibility for another's welfare, strengthening and maintaining relationships, focus on attachment/ abandonment, knowing the particularities of another in his or her own context, and similar considerations (Brown et al., 1988; Gilligan, 1982). The care perspective states that moral issues are not dichotomies of either-or choices; they are struggles to be in relation and to respond in context to particularities. While Kohlberg's justice separates and cuts moral decisions in pieces for making moral action choices, Gilligan's care weaves a web as a way of catching relationships and particularities for making moral action choices.

The methodological differences between Kohlberg and Gilligan's theories are not limited only to the moral domain, but are characteristic of research programs of the 1950s, 1960s, and 1970s. The complexity and richness of narrative and interconnectedness of meanings has characterized research in the 1980s and 1990s. The revolution in research has been in large measure due to Gilligan's influence as well as the concomitant evolution of feminist methodology. As such, it becomes less plausible to talk of one or another moral domain, or of one moral orientation, as being subsumed by or included within the other. I propose that we cease looking at morality through two different lenses with the occasional overlap of lenses. In looking at real life moral issues, there is a tendency to look at the moral decision making process as either justice or care with one predominant viewpoint or with the viewpoints "aligned" with self. One paragraph in the Brown et al. (1988) reading guide suggests that people may use both justice and care in their dilemma considerations. They do this by using the considerations of justice and care side by side, or expressing a tension between the two concepts, or their being "integrated." When people use justice and care in an integrated way, they are said to "create new meanings or to represent conflicts and solutions to conflicts that would not be possible with either voice alone" (Brown et al., 1988, p. 135). Should this *not* be the case? Wouldn't there be a richer conceptualization of morality if people used both orientations?

MORAL DEVELOPMENT AS A PROCESS

What do college students consider to be moral dilemmas? How do they reason about them? What I think needs to be examined in our future study of moral reasoning is the *process* by which people construct a meaningful moral system that struggles with moral conceptualizations of all forms and types. It is extremely useful to use the college student population for this purpose due to their concentrated conscious struggle to develop their moral system. Using current methods of moral research, we tend to examine and value the end-product in the study of moral development, namely, the moral reasons used and action chosen. We ask what considerations were used and how people and relationships were considered. These questions do not belong to either Kohlberg or Gilligan exclusively, but to both. I think that these questions give us important and valuable information about justice or care orientations and moral stage. But there seems to be much more "going on" than that.

In order to better illustrate what I mean by attending to the process of morality and *its* development, I will use a simple example from my everyday life as a metaphor. We have a wall in our family room for displaying artwork. My 5-year-old daughter, Lauren, wishes to have her work displayed more prominently on the wall than that of her 2-year-old sister, Katherine. Lauren believes that only her artwork should be displayed because it is "more beautiful" and that Katherine's work is only "scribble-scrabble."

In discussing the display of artwork, I talk with Lauren about many things, among them, issues of fairness, caring, and development. I remind her that both girls are my daughters and I am proud of both girls' work, and how equally sharing the wall space is just and fair. I talk about issues of care and how I love both daughters, their work, and their feelings, and how I wish to support their sense of pride and encourage their artistic and self-development and their knowledge of being loved and accepted just as they are. I also talk of how I used to display Lauren's scribble-scrabble when *she* was 2. Yet within this discussion I am aware that it is the *result* of the artwork that we're discussing—what the artistic efforts yielded. An artist is engaged in the process of creating. One may have better motor skills, or more artistic talent, or greater perceptual sensitivity, or more practice with art media (e.g., crayons, glue, paint) than another. Should we, as the honored recipients of the artwork, devalue a gift of art because it is more novice than another? Should we not recognize that Katherine is on her way along the journey followed by all developing artists, and appreciate and honor what goes into her efforts, as well as the product of them?

Both girls take obvious pride in their work. They create their art for their own expression of self, are proud of their work, and wish it placed where it can be enjoyed by others. Thus their art is not done solely for the sake of doing it, but also for the sense of joy that comes from sharing the work with other people. It is this interaction or sharing with other people and with society that helps create and shape larger meaning, perhaps leads the artist to create more "realistic," art or that which is more certain to be acknowledged generally as "good." I value both girls' artwork, for what goes into it and for what results. I value the "scribble-scrabble" because of the sense of joy and pride Katherine demonstrates when expressing herself on the paper, when she lifts the completed project in her tiny hands and toddles across the room boasting, "Look, Mommy, I made a picture! Hang it on the wall in the family room!" (she is very verbal). She created this product for herself, but also for another. I recognize that not all will find Katherine's scribbles as enchanting as I do. Certainly they are not museum pieces, and certainly she does not find the same sense of connection in showing the picture to a stranger as she does in showing it to her mother. But should her work enjoy on the art wall in our home similar prominence to that of Lauren's expressions of flowers and rainbows? If we value the process of creating and recognize the meaning that is held for the creator and the one with whom that creation is shared—the processes of self integrity and being in relation—then both girls' artwork ought to be represented.

Like this artwork, morality needs to be examined in terms of both the process and the product: a process, in the making, comprising various skills, methods, perceptions, and sensitivities, done for the self by the self, and done by the self in relation to others. We must recognize, too, that we all reach out to others and consider them in the process of creating moral meaning and in the products created (specifically, the content and structure of moral reasoning and moral choices).

In the moral domain, we must value the processes used to create a moral endpoint—a moral action. The process of getting to moral action may consist of different media (justice or care perspective, stage, and so forth), utilized in different ways, depending on the social and cognitive skills and experiences of the moral decision-maker/actor. But to classify and analyze whether it is justice *or* caring or some predominant or aligned view, or whether it is of one structure of moral perspective-taking or another, simplifies the matter. We enjoy masterpieces when we stand back and appreciate the complexity of the line, the media, the form—how all aspects come together to form the image we call "art." By standing close to examine individual brushstrokes and the mix of color on the canvas, we see the techniques employed, but lose an important dimension of the painting. In morality, we have categorized and analyzed using false dichotomies and excluded the importance of aspects of the "other" perspective by "subsuming" one within another or rejecting the structural components of development. Instead of using two lenses to look at moral orientation, we must begin to look at morality as a kaleidoscope in which the various issues, norms, elements, considerations, voices, or perspectives can be seen working together, ever changing, complementing each other, and providing a more complete view of the thoughts and actions of people as they struggle with moral issues in all their complexity.

COLLEGE STUDENTS' MORAL DILEMMAS

To illustrate this complexity, this chapter examines real life dilemmas—the strategies and resolutions of college students. Sixty-five students participated in an interview study. These students represented a cross section of all 4 years in college, were aged 18–22, and were equally distributed by class and gender. The volunteers came from large lecture classes that draw from throughout a large research university, representing many diverse majors and colleges. The interview consisted of Form B of Kohlberg's Moral Judgment Interview (Colby & Kohlberg, 1987) and Gilligan's (1982) real life interview, and metacognitive questions about how students thought about their moral thinking while resolving these dilemmas (Schrader, 1988).

Content analysis of the nature of the dilemmas students face revealed nine categories of moral dilemmas. The greatest number of students reported dilemmas involving close personal relationships (n=14) and cheating/stealing (n=14). These were not gender-related. Ten student dilemmas focused on issues related to keeping relationships such as those in which they were talking with someone about their behavior, specifically about issues of drug and alcohol use, eating disorders, hazing, or talking behind someone's back. Other relationship-maintaining moral issues involved keeping a verbally abusive friend or a cheating friend, or a friend who had become brain-damaged. The 14 students who discussed cheating/stealing discussed stealing food, software, another's work, or company time to do one's schoolwork. Cheating dilemmas centered around discussing a take-home exam, getting extra points on a misgraded test, cheating in a tennis match, voting in a student election too many times, writing another's personal statement for graduate school, cutting in line in the cafeteria, or not telling about hitting another person's car. Also under this category fell the dilemma of reporting an unliked person for cheating, stealing a test, or taking drugs. Thus, on its face, it seems that the justice and care issues prevail: that the relationship dilemmas support a moral conception of care and response, while the cheating/stealing dilemmas support a moral conception of justice—at least, in terms of what is identified as a moral problem. What becomes muddled is how those dilemmas are understood by the individuals. In the dilemma that involved reporting the bad behavior of an unliked person, for example, the justice and care issues were unclear even for the participant. It could be a justice dilemma as to whether one ought to report cheating, but could also be a caring one in which one would respond differently to a liked person than to an unliked person. Or it could involve the justice quality of universality, such that one ought to report all people who cheat, regardless of their likability or any future relationship one might have with them. Or, should one not report the unliked person because that person would share future classes with them for the remainder of their programs, thus allowing for some consideration of a future, possibly different relationship together? All these considerations were articulated by the participant in the interview. Is the person's response justice oriented? Care oriented? Which predominates? Aligns with self? Are they integrated? What is the person's moral judgment stage? These questions could probably be answered with current "reading guides" and scoring systems, but what do they tell us about the texture and quality of the person's struggle with moral issues? What do they tell us about the inner experiencing of the struggle to balance and make sense of the moral world and how the self is acting in it? Where is the sense of the person *creating* a moral product, an outcome, or a moral action that she or he wants to point to and say, "I made this!" Other types of dilemmas students struggled with include Personal Issues (n = 9), such as being politically involved, going to a party, taking a job, taking drugs, and supporting another's moral decision. Other students discussed Authority Issues (n = 8), such as breaking with cultural, family, or legal rules (drugs, sex, curfew, living at home); telling parents on a sibling; or reporting an incompetent teacher. Infidelity Issues were salient for seven participants. These involved telling on another's infidelity, being asked to lie for another, and being unfaithful. Four participants talked about Greed: keeping money they scalped from selling a ticket given by a friend, taking too much food at the co-op, transferring to another college to make more money, or continuing in an unfair living arrangement. Four additional participants faced a classical dilemma categorized here as Life (n = 4): euthanizing a pet, or participating in a decision about euthanizing a family member. Peer Pressure (n = 3) to take drugs, a job, or beer presented dilemmas, and Respect (n = 2)—defined by college students as taking revenge on someone who "disrespected" them—complete the set of dilemmas presented by this college student sample. (Note that these categories were developed based on how the student chose to construct or frame the dilemma, so some of the brief descriptions within the category might sometimes seem to fit into more than one category. The predominant presenting issue was used to construct the category.)

Resolutions

The most oft-used strategies for resolving these dilemmas involved considering consequences to the self, one's own feelings, and rationalizing decisions that required immediate (as opposed to reflected upon) resolutions. Some students used strategies that considered consequences to others as well as to the self, and talking with others or obtaining other opinions. Distraction strategies, such as "getting away" emotionally or mentally from the problem; logical/rational strategies, such as lists of pros and cons; impulse or passion—"if it feels good, do it," and the "easiest thing to do"—strategies were also frequently used. A few cases used strategies such as reversibility, or considered society's rules and/or one's own morals. What is "practical," doing what one felt "forced" to do because of feeling helplessness in the situation, or deciding based on past experience were also considerations for a few students.

When it came time for action, most cases resolved the dilemmas by letting the issue drop, by doing nothing, by going along with the situation or with others in it, and by letting the problem resolve itself somehow. Or students went along with "what they thought was right," which included acting on gut reactions, immediate answers that "popped" into their heads, and what "felt right." Another way students used to resolve a situation was in terms of self-interest—what felt good or would avoid pain or punishment to the self.

These strategies for resolving the moral problem again demonstrate the complexity of students' thought processes and their struggles in working with moral issues. Going back to the art metaphor, students seem to have all the materials they need for creating their moral pictures, but might not have the fully developed ability to put these media (the moral elements and social-moral-cognitive system) together to make a beautiful moral picture—that is, to use well the elements of morality (justice and care), coordinate their cognitive and moral skills, and apply them well to create a good moral outcome. Doing so required developing sensitivity to moral issues, perspective-taking skills, and experience or practice with confronting and thinking about moral issues and dilemmas. These students are clearly not the moral equivalent of Rembrandt, but we *can* attend to students' processes of moral meaning making and honor their struggle to create moral meaning.

In the simplest sense, Kohlberg's moral stages could define most of the egocentric and individualistic consequences considerations seen in the above resolution strategies as Preconventional, or lacking in reversibility and coordination of consequences of self and other, and define the considerations of self and society's morals as Conventional. Alternatively, Gilligan's theory might consider the resolution strategy of talking with others and considering consequences to self and other as exemplifying the care orientation, and those resolutions based on logic and rationality as exemplifying the justice orientation. But of course one would need the full interview transcript to discern which. My point here is that these strategies that students use are too rich to distill into a dichotomous category, or to juxtapose an orientation with a stage assignment. It is useful and instructive for work with college students to see what goes into identifying and constructing a moral problem, and to examine the realities of students' thinking about it. Making decisions because one runs out of time or runs away from the problem isn't justice or caring, but it is a reality in the moral psychology of smart college students who have been taught skills to analyze academic issues but not moral ones.

An Example

The following example illustrates the complexity of college students' moral experience. The contents of the dilemma presented are not meant to illustrate exemplary moral reasoning of any sort, but rather what is involved in the process of moral decision making in college students. I wish to call attention to three things: (1) the real struggles this person is going through, (2) how we as moral theorists react to the dilemma and the reasoning process this person uses, and (3) the question of adequacy of the use of moral stage and justice or care orientations for understanding the process of constructing of a value and belief system in which this person is actively engaged.

"Pat" (a pseudonym) reported the following moral dilemma, which happened at the end of the academic year. Pat's friends made arrangements to meet him at a bar at a particular time. Pat forgot which bar and subsequently missed connecting with his friends and so went home to sleep. He had planned to leave Ithaca early the following morning and was anxious to do so. At about 1:10 A.M., Pat received a call from these friends, who were angry at the missed meeting, and Pat was equally angry at having missed them, so all agreed to get together at one person's apartment to "just talk or whatever." When Pat arrived, the friend said, "Well, where are we going to get some beer?" and Pat suggested that the local grocery store would probably still be open.

When Pat arrived at the store and attempted the purchase, the clerk notified Pat that beer could not be sold after 1:00 A.M. Pat's friends did not welcome this news and said, "Well, looks like you're going to have to stick around. Since you didn't get your beer, you're just going to have to stick around for another day, and you're going to have to party with us tomorrow night." Pat said, "No, no way. I'm not going to stick around here any longer. I can't do this." Pat went to another store and found that the beer was in a freezer area that had an alarmed door to the outside. Pat grabbed a 12-pack of beer, opened the door, and jumped into the car, saying, "Take off. Go, go!" and they returned to the apartment. Pat concluded, "So I got away with getting some beer and we had some beer that night, and I was able to leave in the morning. So I was forced with a decision to either do something wrong and steal a 12-pack of beer, or stick around in Ithaca when you don't want to and party with these people."

When asked what the moral issue was, Pat said, "The moral issues? You stole a beer. The moral issues was [sic] I sacrificed my integrity or whatever to do something. I did that in order that I wouldn't have to go through—I wouldn't say a painful experience, but go through an experience I didn't want to go through." Pat said he felt forced in the situation, as though the decisions and situations were not controlled by the self but by others. He said that this was a violation of his integrity because of the need to avoid doing what he didn't *want* to do—namely, stay in Ithaca for another day.

How do our moral theories make sense of Pat's thinking? What orientation was used, justice or care? What did Pat consider to be morally right? According to Pat, it was not personal integrity, nor the law against stealing (justice considerations), nor the need to be connected and maintain the relationships with friends (care considerations). What was right was doing whatever it took to attain a goal. Is this kind of thinking about self separate or connected? Pat was an independent moral actor in deciding to steal the beer and did not consider others in doing so (that is, in involving them in a theft), but the *motivation* for doing so emanated from responding to others and the context of the situation. Pat's reasoning had some traces of duty and commitments to others. Pat felt an obligation to "party" with these friends before leaving town, or such drastic actions would not have ensued. In Pat's mind, "connections of interdependent individuals to one another" or "promoting the welfare of others" or "relieving burdens, hurt, or suffering" might have been there, but in a form we as moral theorists might consider "messy" at the least. For Pat, the friends' request/demand to party together before Pat left was a strong consideration in the action solution to the dilemma. The evaluation of the decision likewise involved justice and care: Pat used a type of justice evaluation in deciding whether the right moral action was taken in this dilemma, specifically, whether "values, principles, or standards were maintained," but this "standard"—doing what Pat *wanted to do*—was not based on moral principle. Pat also said that personal integrity was a consideration in the evaluation of the resolution to the dilemma, but this, too, did not have a moral flavor to it. Pat thought the solution to steal the beer was right and fair because everyone got what he wanted in the end and no one was arrested. Yet this evaluation and resolution might also be characteristic of a care and response orientation, since relationships were maintained and restored by everyone getting what he wanted—to be together for one last night, and for Pat to leave town only after that.

In Pat's mind, this was a real moral dilemma. In the interview Pat reported thinking about what is right, what gets everyone's needs met, what maintains personal integrity and friendships. Maybe Pat was rationalizing or justifying the action taken. In any case, Pat's reasoning may be what we might call the moral equivalent of scribble-scrabble, to return to the art metaphor. This is exactly what happens in many moral dilemmas college students face. Even though moral psychologists and philosophers might label this as somehow "pathetic," I believe that it is the dilemma itself or the fact that this kind of behavior goes on that is "pathetic"—but not Pat's or any other student's struggle. What Pat illustrates here is a kind of dignity, not unlike the dignity that we accord a young child learning to read or draw or try any new skill. In young children we appreciate the process of becoming. We appreciate that there is a struggle, that the outcome will not be perfect, that sometimes it will be a *mess*. Pat's reasoning here is that kind of mess. While we find such thinking and conclusions to be morally reprehensible—like stealing or getting drunk—that is the reality of many college students' moral lives; this is their moral psychology. While we would all wish for a different outcome, that different outcome needs to arise from some practice at making moral messes and mistakes.

The dilemma Pat presents is not a juxtaposition of two deontic moral rights, as Kohlberg constructs. It is not a conflict of maintaining and strengthening relationship or connections, as Gilligan portrays. Involved in most moral issues college students face are concerns that involve both relationships and caring, and rights, duties, and obligations. People do not have an easy time selecting between these two kinds of moral considerations, primarily because many dilemmas are not easily characterized as justice or caring. Most dilemmas involve both kinds of issues, and can be thought about from many—even opposing—perspectives simultaneously. Forcing moral psychology to look at a predominant orientation misses the richness of understanding how care is used when considering justice issues from various sociomoral perspective-taking viewpoints, and vice versa. Pat's reasoning was preconventional, in Kohlberg's terms, which guided the action and reasoning to be self-interested. Maybe it is the overriding consideration, as Kohlberg might say. But looking at the dilemma as just or caring or preconventional doesn't help Pat think of new approaches to moral thinking or moral action, nor does it provide us with insight into how this person can become a contributing citizen, a caring parent, or a moral person.

What the field of moral psychology needs to do is to try to understand how students struggle to conceptualize morality. How do they learn to think about what is right, virtuous, valuable? What are the mental demands of the college context that creates such challenges for students that they are stymied in their thinking about moral issues and opt for self-interest and/or responding to others' desires?

The challenge for moral development researchers is to look at the integrity in the struggle for college students to create a moral system that they can share proudly, like a child's art project, with the world. This requires a shift in the current state of moral research. We must cease the dichotomization of two separate lines of moral inquiry and look at these issues in their context and with the complexity and richness they deserve.

IMPLICATIONS FOR FUTURE RESEARCH AND EDUCATION

The research on justice and care perspectives has been useful thus far in that such enterprises have allowed further examination and articulation of the domain of moral psychology. What needs to occur in the next phase of research is to create the equivalent of a "meta-theory" (Kegan, 1982) of moral psychology—one that includes a perspective on and synthesis of the Kohlberg and Gilligan enterprises. This will not be easy, since the research enterprises stem from different paradigms and speak different languages. Yet this is again an example of the "messy-ness" that I suggest we consider in individuals' moral reasoning; we need to extend our tolerance for such things until we as moral researchers can construct a new way of examining the field that transcends our current perspective on it.

Seeing imperfect or messy moral reasoning, such as that of college students, may be useful in several ways. One is that through such chaos in thinking, new possibilities are created. Another is that tolerance of what might seem to some to be "pathetic" dilemmas or reasoning may help get us closer to the way people actually construct their moral psychology, and not limit us to descriptions of moral reasoning such as stage and orientation. Rather, we can get closer to the psychological processes used in constructing reasoning or moral orientation. In addition, this "messy-ness" may help our understanding of the processes of moral stage transition as well, and give implications for new strategies of moral education that promote conscious reflection and experimentation—sometimes with paradoxical moral issues, considerations, and contexts.

I believe that the messy-ness or confusion that was illustrated here by Pat's thinking is to be honored as a way of thinking in that it helps us as researchers to notice the very basic elements involved in moral psychology. Note that I am not saying that Pat's moral reasons or decisions were moral or exemplary—rather, I am referring to the process of the struggle. It provides a chance to get at the very heart of the field. Perhaps what is needed is to take these responses to moral situations and give them more weight; look at what these things tell us about how to construct a moral system or to live a moral life. We need to recognize that this is part of life and essential to gaining increased understanding of moral psychology. Again, as with children's art, we need to consider the development of technique, and the choice of subjects and material used, and recognize the gradual process that is involved in making use of moral talents, perceptions, sensitivities, and growing social-cognitive skills.

From an educational standpoint, what can be gained by looking at a process perspective to morality and a synthesis of justice and care? One suggestion is that the moral life should not be treated as separate from issues addressed at home, in school, and in society. It is impossible to have a complete picture of moral thoughts and actions when we artificially dissect contexts of human existence. Both Nel Noddings (1992) and Jane Roland Martin (1992) propose looking at education as a complex process and not a product, and advocate developing exercises that recognize that students are complex people who grow best in conditions that provide support and encouragement, make connections between subject matter and life, and use dialogue and conversation. They both encourage practice as well. Practice is needed to help students be open and receptive to others in their humanness, and to encourage the best in others. As researchers, we need to do the same in our study of morality.

Fritz Oser (1990) articulates various forms of educational engagement, but advocates a perspective that he derived from Kohlberg's educational theory. Specifically, teachers—and I add, moral researchers—ought to engage in what he calls "Discourse II": where the teacher "accepts personal responsibility for settling a problem and subscribes to the task of balancing justice, care, and truthfulness in each new situation . . . is committed to a good life and a just environment," *and* in addition "presupposes that each student (and any other person who is involved) is, in a deep sense, a rational human being who is also interested in and capable of balancing justice, care and truthfulness" (p. 86). Oser called Kohlberg's educational approach a "developmental approach embedded in to a social participatory fabric of our everyday life" (p. 81). This, I think, captures the vision of what a new understanding of morality must be—something that reflects the complexity of everyday life, and recognizes transformations of thought and self in the context of experience and interactions with others. I do not think Kohlberg and Gilligan were misguided. We simply need to permeate the boundaries of the systems they created, moving across and between systems to acknowledge the strengths and weaknesses, and the interdependence of concepts about morality that each discovered, and create a new system. Dialogue with real people and opening our minds to divergent theoretical perspectives is key, as is attending to the process and not only the products (stages, orientations) of moral reasoning.

The challenge for moral psychology is to understand the complexity of the interconnections between self and morality, between justice and care, and between reason and motivation. It is through dialogue and the recommendations presented above, and through a better understanding of how individuals develop self-conscious reflective awareness, that the picture of the moral domain can be more complete.

Acknowledgment. I wish to thank Scott D. Hill and Bill Puka for helpful comments on an early draft of this paper.

REFERENCES

Attanucci, Jane. (1988). In whose terms: A new perspective on self, role and relationship. In Carol Gilligan, Janie Ward, & Jill Taylor (Eds.), *Mapping the moral domain* (pp. 201–224). Cambridge, MA: Harvard University Press.

Baumrind, Diana. (1986). Sex differences in moral reasoning: Response to Walker's conclusion that there are none. *Child Development, 57,* 511–521.

Beilin, Harry. (1992). Piaget's new theory. In Harry Beilin & Peter Pufall (Eds.), *Piaget's theory: Prospects and possibilities.* Hillsdale, NJ: Erlbaum.

Blasi, Augusto. (1990). Kohlberg's theory and moral motivation. In Dawn Schrader (Ed.), *The legacy of Lawrence Kohlberg* (pp. 51–57). San Francisco: Jossey Bass.

Boyd, Dwight. (1981). The condition of sophomoritis and its educational cure. *Journal of Moral Education, 10*(1), 24–39.

Brown, Lyn et al. (1988). *A guide to reading narratives of conflict and choice for self and moral voice.* Unpublished manuscript, Harvard University.

Colby, Anne, & Damon, William. (1992). *Some do care: Contemporary lives of moral commitment.* New York: Free Press.

Colby, Anne, & Kohlberg, Lawrence. (Eds.). (1987). *The measurement of moral judgment.* New York: Cambridge University Press.

Gibbs, John, Arnold, Kevin, & Burkhart, Jennifer. (1984). Sex differences in the expression of moral judgment. *Child Development, 55,* 1040–1043.

Gilligan, Carol. (1977). In a different voice: Women's conceptions of the self and of morality. *Harvard Educational Review, 47,* 481–517.

Gilligan, Carol. (1982). *In a different voice: Psychological theory and women's development.* Cambridge, MA: Harvard University Press.

Johnston, Kay. (1988). Adolescents' solutions to dilemmas in fables: Two moral orientations—two problem solving strategies. In Carol Gilligan, Janie Ward, Jill Taylor (Eds.), *Mapping the moral domain* (pp. 49–72). Cambridge, MA: Harvard University Press.

Kegan, Robert. (1982). *The evolving self: Problem and process in human development.* Cambridge, MA: Harvard University Press.

Kohlberg, Lawrence. (1984). Synopses and detailed replies to critics. In *The psychology of moral development*, Volume 2 (pp. 320–386). San Francisco: Harper & Row.

Lyons, Nona. (1982). *Conceptions of self and morality and modes of moral choice: Identifying justice and care in judgments of actual moral dilemmas.* Unpublished doctoral dissertation, Harvard University, Cambridge, MA.

Lyons, Nona. (1983). Two perspectives: On self, relationships, and morality. *Harvard Educational Review, 53*(2), 125–145.

Martin, Jane Roland. (1992). *The schoolhome: Rethinking schools for changing families.* Cambridge, MA: Harvard University Press.

Noddings, Nel. (1992). *The challenge to care in schools: An alternative approach to education.* New York: Teachers College Press.

Oser, Fritz. (1990). Kohlberg's educational legacy. In Dawn Schrader (Ed.), *The legacy of Lawrence Kohlberg* (pp. 81–87). San Francisco: Jossey Bass.

Piaget, Jean. (1965). *The moral judgment of the child.* New York: Free Press. (Original work published in 1932).

Puka, Bill. (1991). Interpretive experiments: Probing the care-justice debate in moral development. *Human Development, 34*, 61–80.

Schrader, Dawn E. (1988). *Exploring metacognition: A description of levels of metacognition and their relation to moral judgment.* Unpublished doctoral dissertation, Harvard University.

Tappan, Mark, Kohlberg, Lawrence, Schrader, Dawn, & Higgins, Ann. (1987). Heteronomy and autonomy in moral development: Two types of moral judgments. In Anne Colby & Lawrence Kohlberg (Eds.), *The measurement of moral judgment* (pp. 315–380). New York: Cambridge University Press.

Walker, Lawrence. (1984). Sex differences in the development of moral reasoning: A critical review. *Child Development, 55*, 677–691.

Walker, Lawrence. (1986). Sex differences in the development of moral reasoning: A rejoinder to Baumrind. *Child Development, 57*, 522–526.

Walker, Lawrence, de Vries, Brian, & Trevethan, Shelley. (1987). Moral stages and moral orientations in real-life and hypothetical dilemmas. *Child Development, 58*, 842–858.

PART II

Pedagogical Issues

CHAPTER 4

Teaching About Caring and Fairness: May Sarton's *The Small Room*

Michael S. Katz

In attempting to provide prospective teachers with a heightened awareness of their moral responsibilities, for the past decade I have had students interpret May Sarton's novel *The Small Room* (1961/1976) to highlight a fundamental tension in teaching: the tension between being a caring person and being a fair-minded one. By using a complex novel to raise moral awareness, I have implicitly suggested that treating others well, in a way both caring and fair, may not be a straightforward affair of principled reasoning, but rather a matter of acting out one's character in a messy situation. In so doing, one's conduct reveals how one understands or misunderstands others, reads situations well or badly, and sometimes just "muddles through" using one's moral intuitions as well as possible. In good novels, a fundamental opacity accompanies how characters make decisions and understand what these decisions mean, since literature reveals experience indirectly through figurative language, symbolism, metaphorical descriptions, and dramatic dialogue. Rather than being told discursively what is more or less important, a novel's readers are being shown how things are; moreover, characters are portrayed as complex individuals acting out their own conscious and subconscious motives, interpreting or misinterpreting themselves and others in the process, and sometimes changing as a result of new insight into themselves. Indeed, one central theme in literature is that the wisdom acquired by a protagonist in confronting a major conflict leaves that person changed;

he or she emerges somehow as a different person after the conflict has been resolved because his or her view of the world has been altered as a result of what has happened. So it is with Lucy Winter's journey into and through the plagiarism crisis that accompanies her first months of teaching at Appleton, an elite all-girls college in New England.

In *The Small Room*, Lucy Winter, a first-year English teacher, finds that one of her most brilliant students, Jane Seaman, has plagiarized a Simone Weil essay interpreting the *Iliad*. However, Lucy must not only respond to the student's act of plagiarism, but must also deal with the student's brilliant mentor, Carryl Cope, who has championed this student and whose personal reputation and judgment will be scrutinized in the college community if the student's plagiarism becomes public. The challenge for the reader is not merely to interpret how well Lucy balances caring and fairness in handling the plagiarism incident and its messy aftermath, but also to grasp what it means for any first-year teacher to grapple with one's moral responsibility to others, to oneself, and to one's community.

In responding to a novel, the reader is invited to participate imaginatively in the story and to respond emotionally as well as rationally to the moral situation in all of its three-dimensional complexity. In my view, one thing that makes teaching moral understanding through literature so compelling is that the complexity of interpretation renders thoughtful disagreement about moral character and morally responsible conduct unavoidable. Good novels seem consistently to bring about the following educational condition: reasonable students *disagree* about "what is going on" in a messy situation and *disagree* about "what is at stake in treating others well." Exploring the reasons underlying these disagreements is what makes teaching these issues so rewarding.

Thus, in teaching May Sarton's novel, I have been able to ask questions that live outside and inside the novel itself. These include:

What does it mean to be a caring person?
Should we expect teachers to be caring toward their students?
Are there different ways of conceiving of fairness?
What does it mean to act fairly in a case of cheating?
How might we distinguish between procedural and substantive fairness in a case of plagiarism?
What possible tension might exist between being caring and being fair?
Must this tension exist?
Should teachers establish close personal relationships with their students?
What is at stake in becoming a moral teacher?

Now, these questions are naturally transformed by the context of the novel; they must be thoroughly contextualized in terms of character and situation, and the layers of complexity—both in terms of character and situation—make the abstract questions take on rich new meaning.

I plan in this chapter to do two things: (1) show how May Sarton's novel *The Small Room* dramatizes the issue of balancing "caring and fairness" in Lucy's handling of the plagiarism incident, and (2) suggest how the novel communicates its own thematic messages to the readers about what is at stake in becoming a moral teacher.

THE TENSION BETWEEN CARING AND FAIRNESS

At the core of teacher-student relations, I believe, is a potential tension between two different moral orientations that are bound up with a teacher's effort to treat students well—the tension between being fair and being caring. What seems to be at stake in these two different orientations? One way to view the tension is as follows: to be a fair judge as a teacher involves making judgments of students' conduct and academic performances without prejudice or partiality; most of the time, it involves the impartial application of appropriate standards to this conduct. In contrast, to be a caring person, one must accept the unique "otherness" of a student in a receptive, supportive, open, and essentially *nonjudgmental* way. Judging students fairly is bound up with the unequal power relationships existing between teachers and students and with one facet of this power relationship—teachers distributing one of education's most precious commodities, grades. It is also bound up with punishment of students for breaking accepted classroom or school rules, such as the rule against plagiarism. Unlike the unequal power relationship of judging, the caring relationship between teacher and student often operates on a level of moral equality, with at least one of the two struggling to understand and support the other in her humanness.

In May Sarton's *The Small Room*, the tension between fairness and caring is revealed through background and foreground problems as well as through several key relationships. One background problem for fairness is: should exceptionally bright students receive special treatment if they break the college's standard rules? An early incident in the novel involves the faculty's decision of whether or not to suspend a brilliant math student who has failed to come to class or turn in her work for weeks; the faculty deliberates in a public meeting over whether exceptional intellectual talent should be taken into account if a student breaks the conventional rules. This incident provides a "fairness backdrop" to the Jane Seaman plagiarism case. Both students are brilliant and break college rules; both cases ultimately have to be decided by faculty and students. Similarly, there exists a background problem for caring: should Appleton College hire a psychologist to treat students with emotional problems?

Closely connected to this background problem of appointing a school psychologist is the central philosophical problem of what is involved in "educating a person." Is education primarily a matter of cultivating intellectual excellence? Or is it something more? Might it be something bound up with the whole person, with a healthy psyche or a spiritually nourished soul? The problem of "what it means to educate a person," of course, is not an abstract intellectual problem in a novel; rather, it is built dramatically into a core relationship, the relationship between Lucy Winter and Carryl Cope, both of whom will anguish over how to be both fair and caring with Carryl's protégé, Jane Seaman, the senior who commits the self-destructive act of plagiarizing an essay and places it into a volume of *Appleton Essays* that Carryl is preparing to publish for the college. For Carryl Cope, education revolves around fostering excellence and paying the price of so doing. For Lucy, whose views are emerging, something is wrong with this view; for her, education comes to mean developing the whole person, emotionally as well as intellectually. Moreover, I wonder whether Jane Seaman's failure, that which led to her act of plagiarism, is more than the case of a teacher demanding too much of an emotionally unstable, brilliant student. Rather, might it be symptomatic of a college that has lost its moral compass and has neglected something fundamental about what is at stake in helping young women flourish as human beings? In other words, might Carryl Cope's failure of caring—the capacity to meet the real needs of a troubled student—be part of the college's misguided overemphasis on the intellect? I raise this as a question of interpretation only. The point here is that the background issue of whether to hire a school psychologist is directly connected to one issue of caring: how do a college and its professors meet the needs of its students, including those who may be emotionally troubled?

The central foreground problem is how Lucy should handle the case of Jane Seaman, the brilliant senior who has plagiarized. This elite women's institution has a clear procedural judicial mechanism for rule violations: a student court and a faculty senate to hear all recommendations for expulsion. It also has a clear substantive punishment for plagiarism: expulsion with no extenuating circumstances. This judicial condition raises the further issues of procedural and substantive fairness. Procedurally, Jane is entitled to be warned of her offense and given a chance to defend herself; in a criminal proceeding she would be entitled to a quick and speedy trial held according to appropriate rules of evidence and procedure and with an impartial judge or jury. These are simply part of her "due process" rights—the essence of her entitlement to procedural fairness. Substantively, we can also ask about fairness or what philosophers call "retributive justice"—how well does the punishment fit the crime? Does expulsion seem warranted for an act of plagiarism, or is the penalty too severe? There is little formal discussion in the novel about retributive justice, but both Lucy Winter and Carryl Cope seem convinced that expulsion of a person with Jane Seaman's intellectual potential would be unfair. The novel raises an additional issue of substantive retributive justice: is expulsion from college the fair response to a girl whose plagiarism seems to be, at the unconscious level, an act of intellectual suicide, a desperate cry for help from someone on the verge of a mental breakdown? The notion of "expulsion without extenuating circumstances" seems to present "fairness" problems here for Jane Seaman and her sympathizers, especially if her act of plagiarism is not simply a blatant form of cheating, but is instead a hidden cry for psychological help.

In many cases in which first-year teachers encounter a case of plagiarism, the teacher is asked to do what is almost impossible from the standpoint of fairness: be simultaneously the prosecuting attorney and the judge. The teacher must investigate the plagiarism, give the student a chance to defend herself, and then render an impartial verdict. In Lucy's case, she need not be the ultimate judge herself, since the student court exists for that. However, she must first decide how to act. Should she do nothing? Go to a colleague to talk it over? Turn the case into the Student Court right away?

Sarton's readers do not experience Lucy agonizing over her first critical decision. She simply acts: she researches the plagiarism, takes her problem to a trusted confidante, Hallie Summerson, a fellow English teacher who is quite close with Carryl Cope, and then confronts the student in her office, a very small room.

To interpret how well Lucy balances the tension between caring and fairness, students in my classes are given background reading on both topics. I have them read my own essay on fairness (Katz, 1990) in which I contrast two versions of fairness: a juror model of fairness emphasizing due process and strict impartiality, and Aristotle's equality version of fairness. In the juror model, the emphasis is on strict impartiality in the unbiased application of appropriate standards; in the Aristotle model, the judge must consider three conditions of fairness: (1) like cases are treated alike; (2) different cases are treated differently; (3) different cases should be treated differently in proportion to the differences at stake. In the Aristotelian model, the burden of proof lies with the person, suggesting that there is a relevant difference, which warrants different treatment. Moreover, I also have them read Milton Mayeroff's classic essay *On Caring* (1971) and some of Nel Noddings's (1984) writings on caring. For example, Mayeroff (1971) suggests that there are three key ingredients in caring: (1) "being with," which involves the empathic ability to put oneself in the other's shoes, see the world through her eyes, without losing one's identity in the process; (2) "being for," which is the opposite of molding or shaping another to live up to one's own expectations or making the other's decisions for her; rather it is the effort to support the other in her efforts to become the kind of person the other chooses to be; (3) "being there for" the other, which involves being "on call" for the other and being willing to rearrange one's priorities to respond appropriately to the other's need, difficulty, or crisis. Nel Noddings's (1984) view of caring substitutes the notion of "engrossment" for empathy and emphasizes the receiving of the other, rather than placing oneself in the other's shoes. Noddings writes: "The commitment to act in behalf of the cared-for, a continued interest in his reality throughout the appropriate time span, and the continual renewal over this span are the essential elements of caring" (p. 16).

Lucy's confrontation of Jane Seaman in chapter 7 dramatizes the initial tension between caring and fairness (Sarton, 1961/1976). It is a scene I have students act out in class to experience the drama of shifting emotions. At the outset of the scene, Lucy is taken aback by Jane's repeated denials of the plagiarism. In the scene, Lucy is "completely baffled" and talks to Jane: "'I didn't ask you here to argue. I wanted to try to help. If you don't wish to discuss it with me, that is surely your right.' Lucy got up to leave. She felt unutterably weary, as if her mouth were filled with ashes. 'Damn it, Jane!' she exploded suddenly, 'Give yourself a chance!'" (p. 96). Lucy is filled with rage and shame and frustration at this point as the student sits there in arrogant, smug denial. By the end of the scene, however, after the student has confessed and explained why she had plagiarized—to escape the increasing pressure after each success—the student is described as follows: "How small, crumpled, and how very young Jane looked, bent over the chair, hugging herself" (p. 104).

In her interrogation of Jane, Lucy has called forth another emotion that has shocked her—Jane's disdain for her mentor, Carryl Cope, with whom Lucy has recently developed an affectionate, albeit ambivalent, relationship. In this scene, the reader can feel how both Lucy and Jane are caught in the middle of their very different relationships with Carryl, virtually the only major research figure at this college and a person whose charismatic personality and powerful campus presence have polarized the entire faculty. Lucy asks Jane somewhat angrily, "Has it occurred to you, Jane, that you are throwing Carryl Cope to the wolves? She gave me that issue of *Appleton Essays* with particular pride." Jane's response is quick and contemptuous: "What a sell for her! The infant prodigy turns out to be a fake" (p. 102).

One interesting twist here is that by the end of the scene, Lucy has taken a thoroughly caring stance toward Jane. Lucy says to Jane, "You've got to go through this now, and it's going to be tough. But you will not be alone, Jane. People care, you know." The narrator adds, "Lucy was surprised to discover that she herself cared more than she would have thought possible a half hour ago" (p. 103). What makes Lucy's shift to a caring stance toward Jane somewhat ironic is that Lucy has prided herself up to this point on keeping a professional distance between her and her students. She has tried not to become emotionally involved with them. In this regard, on two previous occasions she has turned away the pleas for caring from another student in Jane's American literature class, Pippa Brentwood, a young woman who has recently lost her father and desperately seeks an emotionally supportive relationship with Lucy. Lucy's formulaic recipes for dealing with students simply do not work. Caring for Jane is not something Lucy has decided to do; it simply expresses who she is at this point in their mutual crisis. She concludes their confrontation with a willingness to "be there for" Jane. She says to her in parting, "Don't hesitate to come to the Faculty Club any time. I'll always be there if you need me" (p. 104). At the end of this scene, the author tells us that as a result of playing the role of "inquisitor and judge," Lucy's knees are trembling. What the author does not tell us quite so directly is that Lucy has emerged as the person she truly is—a very caring person.

At this point in the novel, one might expect that the plagiarism case would be brought to the student court, that Lucy might even testify in Jane's defense, and that procedural fairness would take over. If such an event had occurred, the novel up to this point might serve in some way *as an extended case study*. What is the proper verdict? How would you decide? Was this something more than cheating? What punishment does Jane Seaman deserve? These are questions one could ask and answer. The problem here is that the novel is not merely about Lucy and Jane Seaman. It centers dramatically on Carryl Cope and her relationships with Lucy and others. Carryl Cope does not understand how the student's plagiarism is an unconscious rejection of her and their one-sided relationship. Thus her first instinct is to protect the student, protect herself, and not have the case go to trial. She has the forty unpublished copies of *Appleton Essays* containing Jane's plagiarized piece recalled. When Lucy sees her the next day, Carryl indicates that she will not permit the case to go to the student court. She tells Lucy, "You thought there were laws, but laws were made for man. My dear Lucy, we cannot afford to have a person of this quality blackballed for life, for that is what it would amount to. We have some human responsibility." Lucy's response astonishes Carryl: "I couldn't agree with you more" (p. 120). Thus, rather unwittingly, *Lucy participates in Carryl Cope's cover-up*. The case does not go immediately to trial. However, since word of Jane's plagiarism leaks out, the students, along with many faculty members, are morally outraged. In addition, Jane is ostracized by the students but shows little outward sign of her inner turmoil. As a result, the mess gets messier.

As readers, what are we to make of Lucy's unwillingness to press the case forward? Why has she let Carryl Cope take control of events in a way that seems so disastrous for all concerned? These questions are never answered directly in the novel. One must read between the lines and speculate. In this regard, something we have learned earlier about Lucy is subtly revealing: as a young girl of 12, she had turned in a fellow classmate, Edna May, for cheating, to her teacher Miss Powers. The author describes the event as Lucy having "set a machinery in motion, and felt the machine get out of control" and characterizes young Lucy as having "carried around the wound of her own righteousness all that year" and having "bitterly despised herself" for so doing (p. 94). Here we see Lucy as someone very uncomfortable turning in another person for wrongdoing. Moreover, throughout the novel the formal procedures of judicial due process at the college are described pejoratively; they are referred to as a process that is cold, impersonal, and cruel, as "the machine," or "the machinery"; the rules are referred to as "the code." When Lucy describes the case as going to the student court, she says, ". . . if I could understand what was back of an act of pure folly [the act of plagiarism] . . . I might be able to help when—in a day or so—the world steps in, the law, the code, the machinery, if you will, takes over" (p. 102).

Lucy's ambivalence about the formal mechanisms of procedural justice and the substantive penalty of "expulsion without extenuating circumstances" lead her not to challenge Carryl's cover-up. At this point, in my view, she has not balanced caring and fairness but has tilted dramatically in the direction of caring. However, another interpretation might be that she just interprets the demands of justice differently; in any case, the demands for formal justice will not readily disappear; quite the contrary, they will be enflamed by the lack of a formal trial. Within a short time, Lucy will be confronted with the effects of the cover-up in the person of Pippa Brentwood, who goes to Lucy full of righteous indignation over what has happened. Pippa, still longing for a caring relationship with Lucy, vents her frustration over Jane's case with Lucy:

> "Miss Winter, I am not a member of student government, but my roommate is. . . . She feels that student government should have been brought in, no doubt. Yes, she does. They criticize you, and Professor Cope. I couldn't stand

it any longer . . . why has it been hushed up? It seems so *unfair*. No one understands. . . . They say it's a pure case of favoritism; if anyone else had done what Jane did, they would have been expelled." (p. 133)

Lucy ends up having an honest, supportive dialogue with Pippa; in it, she challenges some of Pippa's assumptions, defends Jane as a person worth saving, and explains what she thinks might have been Jane's unconscious motivation to Pippa.

> "Here is a girl who has borne the full weight of belief, who has been constantly spurred by a tremendously powerful personality . . . It's possible that Jane couldn't stand the strain this apparently fortunate relationship imposed. I have even imagined—this is pure guesswork—that she stole the essay with the unconscious hope that she would be discovered and so set free. . . . Don't you think that if you were Professor Cope and realized that you had laid a heavy burden on a very young person, had forced her perhaps beyond her strength, that you would wish to take the blame? And if you assumed that responsibility—surely not an ignoble act—would it not be a responsibility toward true justice, not just the pattern of custom or law? Would it be just to punish someone who, instead of punishment, was in dire need of help?" (p. 137)

In this dialogue with Pippa, Lucy justifies Carryl Cope's decision not to bring the case to trial, but in so doing she attributes something to Carryl that may not be the case: Carryl's willingness to take the blame. She has also clearly anticipated the wide-ranging and dangerous consequences that have flowed from Carryl's decision: the ostracism of Jane, the perceived undermining of the student court; and the righteous indignation of both students and faculty over a perceived case of favoritism. Nevertheless, the core of Lucy's view is her final question: "Would it be just to punish someone, who, instead of punishment, was in dire need of help?" What is just or fair here—allowing procedural justice to run its course, or undermining procedural justice to protect a student needing psychological help? Or possibly neither of these? In her justification Lucy suggests that one can contrast a "responsibility toward true justice" with "the pattern of custom or law."

Perhaps, then, it is ironic that the student court and its legal procedures, having been maligned throughout the novel, will produce what is ultimately a very merciful verdict for Jane—allowing her to take a leave of absence for psychological treatment and finish her studies after having done so. Such a verdict is possible only after several intervening events occur: Lucy invites Jane Seaman home with her over Thanksgiving and persuades her to see a psychiatrist; Lucy encourages Pippa to tell her roommate who serves on student government to take the case to the President; and Lucy reports the psychologist's finding that Jane is on the verge of a nervous breakdown in a critical meeting in the President's office prior to a decision about both the trial and the recommendation to the faculty to hire a school psychologist. Throughout this unfolding ordeal, Lucy simultaneously becomes much closer emotionally to Carryl Cope and takes on a new role in relationship to Jane, as a caring adult and defense attorney. Actually, this latter role is assumed shortly after Lucy has confronted Jane about the plagiarism. Lucy tears into her Freshman English class for their terrible papers on *The Iliad*, telling them that their performances could be compared to people standing in Chartres cathedral and remaining unmoved. At the end of her controlled rampage, her freshman applaud Lucy; only then does Lucy realize that something else has been going on while she angrily lectured her freshmen:

> As soon as the spell was broken, she realized that she had spoken as she did, with that violence, because Jane Seaman had been in the back of her mind all the time, Jane's kind of intensity; as if she had been so angry with those freshmen because they would never have the wit to discover Simone Weil's essay, let alone steal from it, as if her burst of rage had been an unconscious defense of Jane. Yes, she saw now, whatever happened in her office the day before, she had *committed herself to the defense.* (p. 109; italics mine)

From inquisitor and judge to defense attorney and caring friend! This is Lucy's journey toward some balance between caring and fairness. What makes the novel so remarkably complicated is that Carryl Cope seems really to be the one on trial, and it is her failed relationship with the student that takes us further in our understanding the challenge of being a caring teacher. Carryl Cope is not the ordinary professor at Appleton. Her presence dominates the entire landscape. We are told that she might have had the Haskins Chair in Medieval History at Harvard, had she been a man. It is she who finds some way to continue doing significant research, writing books and articles, even though this means trips to Europe and the Middle East during her summers. And it is she who embodies the powerful view that the price of intellectual excellence is worth some psychic or emotional maladjustment. In the early incident involving Agnes Skeffington, just as it seems the faculty are favoring expelling the brilliant math student who is working passionately on her own problem rather than attending classes and doing her required academic work, Carryl speaks out persuasively:

> "Let me make it crystal clear that I do not give a hoot whether she comes to my class or not, if she is doing distinguished work in another field. . . . The point is . . . that we talk a great deal about excellence and pride ourselves on

demanding it, but when we get what we have asked for, become as jejune as a freshman in a course on ethics. We are unwilling, evidently, to pay the price of excellence. . . . The price is eccentricity, maladjustment . . . isolation of one sort or another, strangeness, narrowness. Excellence costs a great deal." (p. 69)

The faculty's overwhelming decision to recommend the hiring of a psychologist and to bring the Seaman case to trial is a humbling verdict upon Carryl Cope's decision to protect Jane. It is also a partial rejection of the college's own one-sided emphasis on academic excellence above all. In the penultimate scene, Jennifer Finch, the wise matronly math teacher, tries to explain that something was withheld in Jane Seaman–Carryl Cope relationship that was crucial to its success. Carryl protests: "What in hell did I withhold then? . . . What more am I supposed to give? Time is the most precious thing I have and I gave Jane endless time, time I could not afford, time that should have gone into that long overdue essay for the Seaton Festschrift. . . ." Jennifer continues: "You withheld love" (p. 239).

Carryl admits that Jennifer is right. The irony here is that Carryl, in fact, did love Jane Seaman, cared for her more than she was even capable of admitting to herself. Thus, an element of self-deception, or at least a lack of self-knowledge, was critical to the failed relationship and the cause of so much suffering.

Discussing Carryl Cope within the context of female academics in the 1950s and drawing upon the previous work of Joanne Pagano (1994) and Kathryn Morgan (1987), Barbara Thayer-Bacon (1997) suggests that Carryl Cope was caught "in a double bind" as a senior female professor, expected to be what Kathryn Morgan calls "the bearded mother" by her students, scholastically rigorous and emotionally supportive. Thayer-Bacon writes:

> Carryl Cope was in a no-win situation as a brilliant senior professor in an all-girls school in the 1950s. The double-bind for Carryl Cope is that she is a woman speaking a man's voice to a female student. Rather than Carryl being able to help her student, she causes Jane to feel more like a fraud, and Jane's act of plagiarism becomes just an angry exaggeration of what she suspects she has already been doing. (pp. 224–225)

Neither Carryl Cope nor Jane is able to have the kind of caring relationship Lucy appears to have with both of them. In fact, Lucy emerges as a model of "caring" for Jane, Carryl, and Maria, the wife of foreign language professor Jack Beveridge. Lucy Winter is, using Noddings' terms, able to be "engrossed in" others and to commit herself to their well-being. What she is unable to see, however, is how procedural justice is not necessarily, or even in all probability, incompatible with caring. The notion that Jane could have received a fair trial the first time around seems inconceivable to the central characters. Judicial procedures remain, within the context of this novel, something impersonal and uncaring.

THEMATIC MESSAGES ABOUT BEING A MORAL TEACHER

When I first began thinking about the challenge of educating teachers for moral awareness, I was convinced that the best way to think about this problem was to spell out the kind of role-related obligations teachers had to students both as learners and as persons. Why do that? The answer, I thought, is that being moral should be conceived of primarily as a matter of understanding one's obligations correctly and deliberating appropriately if those obligations should conflict with each other in particular situations. And there is still much to recommend such a view, for as Kenneth Strike and Jonas Soltis (1998) have written elsewhere, achieving a "reflective equilibrium" in which one can balance competing principles in light of specific facts is no small achievement. Judges in courtrooms strive for this kind of reflective equilibrium and the model of tough courtroom cases perhaps best embodies what such a concern for principled decision making consists of. Moreover, judges need not lack compassion or sympathy, but their decisions must be reasoned.

However, there is a competing view of becoming a moral teacher dramatized in Sarton's novel. What *The Small Room* suggests has less to do with good reasoning and more to do with understanding oneself and others in the richly contextualized situations in which we find ourselves. It suggests that somehow our relations with others are primary and that we must discover what these mean as we act out our own character in the world, however confused our sense of our own identity really is. Lucy must simply be the best Lucy Winter she can be as she tries to figure out what it means for her professionally and personally to be a teacher. She cannot be Hallie, or Jennifer, or Carryl. She must simply be *the best Lucy she can be*. And she must try to be honest with herself and others, helping them see her for the person she is. In this regard, she must act courageously on her best intuitions of what is right. She must face the disapproval of those who think she has acted badly but consider the basis of the disapproval. Moreover, what she must recognize is that teaching is not simply about initiating students into subject matter mastery, nor is it about following one's preconceived formulas for establishing an appropriate respectful distance between teachers and students. Teaching, Lucy discovers after her long interview with Jane, is about persons and about relationships, and these are as various as love affairs:

It had been made abundantly clear in the last hour that teaching is first of all teaching a person. Somewhere along the line, someone had failed with Jane. . . . For she had come to see that it was possible, if one worked hard enough at it, to be prepared as far as subject matter went—though Lucy could not imagine such a blessed state—but it was not possible to be prepared to meet the twenty or more individuals of each class, each struggling to grow, each bringing into the room a different human background, each . . . in a state of peril where a too-rigorous demand or an instantaneous flash of anger might fatally turn the inner direction. Was she, for instance, shutting out Pippa's pleas for personal attention and response out of selfishness, fatigue, an unwillingness to give away anything of her inmost heart to a student? How did one know? How did one learn a sense of proportion, where to withdraw, where to yield? And she guessed, not for the first time, that there could be no answer ever, that every teacher in relation to every single student must ask these questions over and over, and answer them differently in each instance, because the relationship is as various, as unpredictable as a love affair. (pp. 104–105)

Where are we left here, then? Is the novel simply recommending a form of situational relativism? The answer is not clear; what is clear is that for Lucy, each situation, each relationship must be interpreted and made sense of in its full contextuality. It cannot be reduced, simplified, or distorted by preconceived recipes or rules of thumb. Such a view does not preclude using principles surely, for Jennifer Finch seems able to do that quite well, but it does seem to prevent them from exercising undue regulatory force. Moreover, it certainly places the student's well-being at the center of the educational process and at the center of moral decision making, but in nothing like a utilitarian calculus.

At another point, Lucy considers whether or not she had taken on more than she could handle in asking Jane to come home with her and see a psychiatrist, and she concludes that what she had done was what all teachers who had really become teachers had to take on: the "care of souls." "Caring for souls" may sound like a very spiritual way of thinking about teaching, but it really is another way of saying that teachers must acknowledge that they are in a special position to help or harm their students. *The Small Room* reveals to us that we have entered into these long-term important relationships with students whether we seek them to be close to us emotionally or not. Students will be relating to us and will be affected by how they do so. In that sense what matters most is not merely what we decide on particular occasions but what kind of person we have become. Teaching, if it is a reflective enterprise, is necessarily an ongoing effort at moral self-improvement. And moral self-improvement is impossible without the continued quest for self-knowledge and the knowledge of others.

Lucy's greatest asset is that she possesses wisdom far beyond her years. It is the wisdom of understanding others and being able to relate to them in caring ways. Where this wisdom has comes from is unclear. What is clear is that it lies at the core of Lucy's ability to treat others well.

Another critical message about becoming a moral teacher conveyed to us by May Sarton's remarkable novel is that we can learn the most from the most adverse situations, situations we would never create for ourselves. When life is most complicated, overflowing with pain and difficulty, we can grow the most. Lucy wanted life to stay simple and manageable, but that was not possible. She wanted to keep students at a distance, not getting involved with them emotionally, but the plagiarism crisis forced her to discover the caring person she truly was. Her confusion and her uncertainty about her personal and professional identity remain with her throughout the crisis, but she finds the courage to act honestly, to be herself. After she overcomes her unease at dealing with Pippa Brentwood's need for emotional support and reveals her uncertainty about how to deal fairly with Jane's plagiarism case, she shakes hands warmly with Pippa, "like two human beings for a change." At this point the author tells us, "And not for the first time that day, she caught herself wondering whether crisis may be one of the climates where education flourishes—a climate that forces honesty out, breaks down the walls of what ought to be, and reveals what *is*, instead" (p. 138).

CONCLUSION

May Sarton's novel *The Small Room* can be interpreted through the lenses of the tension between "caring" and "fairness," and it is through those lenses that I have taught this novel to prospective teachers for the past 15 years. Many students want to deny that there really is a tension between these two values, suggesting that the caring thing is simply to be fair. What seems critical to me, however, is that particular kinds of situations highlight the many-sided features of treating others in both a caring and a fair-minded way. One such situation is that where a teacher's judgment holds a student's future in his or her hands. Because *The Small Room* brings so many of these features into play, I sometimes wonder whether or not I have superimposed a moral structure on the story in a way that obscures other meanings and thematic messages. Perhaps I have. However, from teaching this novel repeatedly and from reading it over and over, I have discovered that one thing has become remarkably clear: the question of what it takes to be a "good" teacher is transformed from an abstract issue into an existential quest for Lucy, just as it is likely to become an existential quest for many of my own prospective teachers.

The novel reminds us that teaching is a messy business because it deals with the fascinating complexity of human relationships. Even the best taught course in the ethics of teaching cannot replace the need for ongoing reflection about how to treat different kinds of people well in different situations. Nor can it supplant the need to penetrate the many blind spots that prevent us from understanding who we are and how we ought to behave. That, for me, is a central message of *The Small Room*. Another is that becoming a teacher is a sacred business; it is about the care of souls, about helping others grow, morally, intellectually, spiritually, and emotionally. Teaching for the Lucy Winters and Carryl Copes and Jennifer Finches and Hallie Summersons of the world can never merely be a job or a profession; it must be, instead, a way of life, a way of being in the world, full of passionate desire, full of uncertainty and anguish, full of the possibility for the most satisfying of human relationships, and fraught with moral complexity. At the core of that moral complexity is the challenge of balancing care and justice.

REFERENCES

Katz, Michael. (1990). The teacher as judge: A brief sketch of two fairness principles. In D. Ericson (Ed.), *Philosophy of education 1990* (pp. 350–359). Urbana: University of Illinois.

Katz, Michael. (1996). Moral stories: How much can we learn from them and is it enough? In Frank R. Margonis (Ed.), *Philosophy of education 1996* (pp. 12–17). Urbana: Philosophy of Education Society and University of Illinois.

Mayeroff, Milton. (1971). *On Caring.* New York: Harper & Row.

Morgan, Kathryn. (1987). "The perils and paradoxes of feminist pedagogy," *Resources for Feminist Research* (16), 49–52.

Noddings, Nel. (1984). *Caring: A feminine approach to ethics and moral education.* Berkeley: University of California Press.

Pagano, Joanne. (1994). Teaching women. In Linda Stone (Ed.), *The education feminist reader* (pp. 252–275). New York: Routledge.

Sarton, May. (1961/1976). *The small room.* New York: W. W. Norton.

Strike, Kenneth, & Soltis, Jonas. (1998). *The ethics of teaching* (3 ed.). New York: Teachers College Press.

Thayer-Bacon, Barbara. (1997). Good stories and moral understanding: Response to Katz. In Susan Laird (Ed.), *Philosophy of education 1997* (pp. 223–225). Urbana: Philosophy of Education Society and University of Illinois.

CHAPTER 5

The Ethical Education of Self-Talk

Ann Diller

Writing in Switzerland during the mid-eighteenth century, Jean-Jacques Rousseau (1762/1911) set down this account of what he called the "natural" relationship between justice and care:

> I would show that justice and kindness are no mere abstract terms, no mere moral conceptions framed by the understanding, but true affections of the heart enlightened by reason, the natural outcome of our primitive affections. (p. 196)
>
> Our first duties are to ourselves; our first feelings are centered on self (p. 61). . . . If the enthusiasm of an overflowing heart identifies me with my fellow-creature, if I feel, so to speak, that I will not let him suffer lest I should suffer too, I care for him because I care for myself. . . . The love of others, springing from self-love, is the source of human justice. (p. 197)

Writing in North America at the end of the twentieth century, Nel Noddings devotes an entire chapter of her book *The Challenge to Care in Schools* (1992) to the topic of self-care. She says: "'Caring for self' is a huge topic. In one sense, everything we care about is somehow caught up in concerns about self" (p. 74). In her earlier work, *Caring* (1984), she makes it clear that proper self-care carries ethical import: "Somehow the child must be led to choose for himself and not against himself, and this means that he will choose not only for his physical self but, more importantly, for his ethical self." (p. 64)

Although Rousseau and Noddings are centuries apart in time, continents apart in space, and paradigms apart in their ethical theories, they both emphasize the centrality of self-care for ethics and moral education. The basic presumption which this chapter takes from them is their observation that self-care, or properly understood self-love, plays a vital role in the development of our sense of ethical justice and our capacity for kindness.

In the spirit of Rousseau I call upon each reader to investigate his or her own experiences in order to observe the interplay between the level of self-care and the sense of justice and kindness toward "fellow-creatures." It is beyond the scope of this chapter to delve into the precise nature of this interplay. For example, I leave it an open question whether there is a mutually interactive process or whether one set of experiences, be it self-love or love for others, tends to "come first" as the more primary source for subsequent development. The key point here is the presumption that self-care carries significant ethical weight. Given this presumption, I want to turn our attention to one specific aspect of self-care, namely that of self-talk.

Self-talk has, I believe, considerable power to enhance or to diminish our ethical selves. In this chapter I propose criteria and strategies to assist us in the ethical education of self-talk so that it might support rather than sabotage morally relevant self-care. My strategies and approach make use of Nel Noddings' ethics of care but also reach beyond it in my investigation of the ethical relevance of self-talk. I consider this exploration to be an extension of Noddings' framework, and not antithetical to it. I do, however, want to allow for a broad interpretation of the term *ethical self* which does not exclude other and various visions of ethical selves. My references to an *ethical self* need not be construed as a metaphysical claim. An *ethical self* can be read simply as a shorthand for ethical aspects of the person, or it can be interpreted in line with Nel Noddings' usage.

SELF-TALK

Since the potential range of possible definitions for *self-talk* looms large, I want to narrow our focus to the sorts of self-talk that show up at the juncture where issues of self-care, education, and ethics all meet. This raises at least two conceptual questions. First, which processes or forms of "articulation" count as instances of self-talk per se? And second, what self-talk content, topics, or subject matter require our attention at this juncture?

When I use the term *self-talk* with educated adults (who are not philosophers) they act, and talk, as if they intuitively know what this means, namely, that self-talk refers to what a person says to herself or himself. The words themselves may be articulated aloud, or muttered sotto voce, or remain "unspoken," yet experienced as accessible within one's conscious awareness. In her book *The Earth House* Jeanne DuPrau (1992) gives vivid accounts of her own self-talk:

> While I work, a commentary proceeds in my head, as if someone in me is worried that I will fail to notice what's going on. It points everything out, like a deranged tour guide. "It's hot!" it screams. "I'm sweaty! This digging stick weighs a ton! Flies are trying to get me! I'm not making any progress! My blisters hurt!" (p. 27)

When I mention self-talk to experienced teachers, especially to coaches, they often go beyond explicitly verbal self-directed commentaries to include guided imagery and visualizations, as when one images herself succeeding in an athletic event. For instance, a competitive skier might visualize herself doing expert turns on a winning ski-run, telling herself how she will handle a difficult turn at high speed. With nonverbal "expressions" such as guided imagery and other visualization practices, the borders of what counts as self-talk become fuzzy and ill defined.

Since visual images do have powerful potential, both ethical and unethical (as in pornography, for example), I do not want to underestimate the importance of scrutinizing these forms of internal self-communication. For many people, internalized words and imagery may feel experientially inseparable; the discernible boundaries between self-directed speech and internal imaging often remain blurred. Nevertheless, the central cases for this chapter will be those more discursive instances of internalized speech that rely primarily on words, or else appear as thoughts and feelings that carry ready potential for translation into words if one paused to verbalize what was "going on inside."

Let us turn now to the second definitional question, namely, what content or subject matter are we talking about here? The answer is that for each of us the subject is myself, my self-image, my activities, my attitudes, any of my thoughts, and my feelings about me. One could use first-, second-, or even third-person forms of self-address. For example, looking in the mirror, I might encourage myself by saying, "You can do it!" or I might criticize myself by saying, "You're a coward." Or I might ask, "Whose face is this that I see in my mirror?"

A pressing postmodern question might now arise, in this context of talking to ourselves about ourselves, namely, to which self are we talking? And most of us need only to "listen" to our internal self-addressed discourses to become perplexed about how we would answer this query, given the increasing awareness of our numerous contingent identities. However, for the purposes of this chapter's investigation, one need not adhere to any particular set of beliefs about the nature, or even about the existence, of the "self" (or selves). For example, one can assume that what most of us call our "self" consists of a series of contingent ever-changing momentary and elusive experiences. We can, in any case, still experience internal self-directed talk.

Whatever theories one may hold about "the self," listening to one's own self-talk leads to the incontrovertible fact that we are besieged by a multiplicity of often contradictory internal voices. DuPrau (1992) captures the phenomenon of self-talk cacophony:

> [My self] changes all the time. . . . It is less like an object than like a space occupied by a jostling crowd. . . .
>   Who are these people that live in my head, then? . . . Some of them are old children—a thousand versions of myself at other ages, myself frozen in a protective reaction to the world. Some are other people. . . . "Be careful!" is the watchword of one of them. "You must find love or you will die," is the refrain of another. Often they come in pairs: "Everything you say is stupid and embarrassing," one says, and its partner, on other occasion, says "You are far smarter than most of those nincompoops out in the world." . . . Each one, in its turn, takes as much of the space as it can grab; it persuades me, while it's front and center, that it is myself. (p. 68)

This extended quotation vividly illustrates the multiplicity of internal voices we can discover if we stop to notice the content of self-directed messages. DuPrau reminds us how much self-talk resembles old internalized replays of other people's voices. A few messages might still be apropos reminders (e.g., "Count to ten before you speak in anger"). Most have outlived their usefulness, if they ever had any, and may contain hurtful self-disparaging content (e.g., "You're a selfish person" or "You're always irresponsible").

Indeed, self-disparaging self-talk attacks are such common occurrences that most educators deplore their untoward effects on students. And teachers often employ a range of stratagems designed to get disparaging self-talk voices out of their students heads, so to speak. The interest that teachers show in students' self-talk is, understandably, in the service of standard educational goals, aimed at helping students to become more successful with the tasks of classroom learning. In most instances the ethical dimensions receive very little, if any, attention. This does not mean that educational approaches have been antithetical to the concerns of ethics, merely that the focus has been elsewhere.

Ethical Import of Self-Talk

When we take up Rousseau's and Noddings' perspectives on the ethical importance of self-care, then self-talk becomes a matter not only of educational concern but also of ethical import. As an ever present aspect of self-care, self-talk matters for these reasons:

1. Our self-talk both manifests and reinforces our beliefs about ourselves as ethical beings. Self-talk is the way we treat, and too often mistreat, ourselves. The tenor and content of self-talk can serve as a barometer indicating one's current level of self-respect. It can also function like a powerful personal atmospheric pressure that sends one's self-respect levels up and down. If, for example, self-talk is demeaning or self-deprecatory, it undermines self-regard and exhibits disrespect toward oneself. But if with one's self-talk she or he can address herself or himself with respect, compassion, and understanding, this can provide a receptive personal space for openness and honesty, thus laying the ground for moral growth based on an accurate, neither vainglorious nor unduly disheartening, sense of one's situation.
2. Our self-talk affects our actions, both directly and indirectly, because what we say to ourselves sets up expectations about our behavior patterns. For example, if I believe I am a cheat, a liar, or an angry or irresponsible person, I may act accordingly, reinforcing my "self-fulfilling prophecies," thus perpetuating unethical patterns of action.

In sum, self-talk can serve either to undermine or to support self-care, which includes care for one's ethical self. If self-talk is to contribute to, and not sabotage, morally desirable forms of self-care, what might this mean for the ethical education of self-talk?

ETHICAL CRITERIA FOR MORALLY GOOD SELF-TALK

What ethical considerations, criteria, practices, or frameworks can help us as educators in working with self-talk so as to support and nourish, rather than undermine, morally relevant self-care?

Turning to Western moral philosophy for assistance in applying ethics to self-talk seems at first glance to provide scarce resources. Furthermore, as Maryann Ayim (1997) notes, it is not merely self-talk that has been neglected; most Western moral philosophers have not given much ethical attention to talk in general, but have limited their attention to a few specific categories of language use, such as "promise keeping, lying, breach of contract, defamation, and misleading advertising" (p. 14), plus, more recently, gossip. In addition to the work of Jurgen Habermas, Ayim's own recent book *The Moral Parameters of Good Talk* (1997) stands out as an exception to the lack in Western philosophy of ethical investigations of talk in general. In this work, Ayim initiates a "sustained discussion of the moral parameters of ordinary conversational exchanges" (p.14). She starts by making a strong case for subjecting much of vocal and written language to moral judgment.

In Chapter 5, Ayim (1997) proposes four "moral criteria of language." She introduces her discussion of the criteria with this statement: "First, morally good language is caring." (p. 98) Ayim's criteria are: (1) language as caring, (2) language as cooperative, (3) language as democratic, and (4) language as honest.

Even though Ayim's moral criteria for delineating the parameters of "good talk" are not designed for self-talk, but rather for "ordinary conversational exchanges" between two or more people, she does provide a framework for subjecting talk in general to ethical scrutiny. In appropriating Ayim's criteria, I focus only on certain similarities between interpersonal "good talk" and ethical self-talk. There are also, of course, significant differences between interpersonal and intrapersonal exchanges. For example, some people's self-talk may invoke idiosyncratic forms of self-castigation that might seem acceptable as self-directed expletives when used in a self-coaching context, yet these same phrases would be considered inappropriate, if not outrageous, when addressed to another person.

Keeping Ayim's four criteria in mind, let us turn to two non-Western traditions on "good talk." First, from the Middle East comes a brief straightforward ethical teaching on when to speak, attributed to the Sufis, who advise us:

> to speak only after our words have managed to pass through three gates. At the first gate, we ask ourselves, "Are the words true?" If so, we let them pass on; if not, back they go. At the second gate, we ask, "Are they necessary?" At the last gate, we ask "Are they kind?" (E. Easwaran, quoted in Houston, 1993, p. 113)

These three Sufi criteria—truth, necessity, and kindness—bear a close resemblance to one set of traditional Buddhist criteria for "Right Speech" translated from the *Vinaya Pitaka*:

> Someone who is about to admonish another must realize within himself [or herself] five qualities before doing so, thus:
> "In due season will I speak, not out of season. In truth will I speak, not in falsehood. Gently will I speak, not harshly. To his [or her] profit will I

speak, not to his [or her] loss. With kindly intent will I speak, not in anger."
(Kornfield 1993, p. 108)

When we compare these three sets of criteria, it is not surprising that
only the twentieth-century Westerner Ayim includes a criterion about being
democratic. Apart from the question of democracy, they bear remarkable
similarities. If we interpret the Sufis' question about whether the words
are "necessary" as following along the same lines as the Buddhist requirements to speak "in due season" and to the other's gain, not to his or her
loss, then these criteria are not unlike Ayim's criterion of "cooperative"
speech. All three agree that the criterion of truth or honesty is a necessary
but not sufficient condition for "right speech." As the Sufis say, truth alone
gets us only through the "first gate."

CARING AND HONESTY IN THE EDUCATION
OF SELF-TALK

It is significant for our purposes to note that in addition to truth or
honesty, all three sets of criteria (Ayim's, Buddhist, and Sufi) invoke some
form of kindness, "kindly intent" or "caring." Thus if one seeks to distill
the essence of these criteria for the purpose of applying them to the ethics
of self-talk, then it seems to me that the conjunction of caring and honesty emerges as central. Let us consider what it might mean to apply the
conjunction of caring and honesty as criteria for morally good talk to the
ethical education of self-talk.
When Ayim discusses her first criterion, she writes:

> If language is caring, it will begin by displaying a readiness to listen to the
> other speakers, and to pay attention to them in verbal and perhaps nonver-
> bal ways. . . . Such behaviour invites others to speak and exhibits a positive
> valuing of their linguistic contributions. (1997, p. 98)

When Nel Noddings (1984) discusses ways of modeling "the ethical ideal
of caring," she writes: "Most important of all, she [the one-caring] listens
to him [the cared-for], and both her listening and her advice are percep-
tive and creative rather than judgmental" (p. 121). To listen to other people
with openness and receptivity is not always easy, yet one can imagine what
it means to give this form of caring attention to another person. Parents,
teachers, good friends, and lovers do, at times, listen this way. When we
shift to the arena of self-talk and ask what it means to do caring nonjudgmental inward listening, it seems less clear how one does this for

oneself or teaches it to others. We may find ourselves agreeing with Eugene Gendlin (1981) that

> most people are pretty unfriendly toward themselves most of the time. If you are like most, you have treated yourself less like a friend than like a roommate you don't like. You grumble at yourself, insult yourself, get impatient with yourself when things go wrong. (p. 80)

To remedy the common tendency toward self-insult, Gendlin (1981) recommends what he calls "The Friendly Hearing" (pp. 80–81). I believe that teachers can and do model forms of "friendly hearing" for their students. In this regard we can perceive the delicate subtleties of caring listening embedded in what appears on the surface to be no more than a simple everyday exchange between a mathematics teacher and one of his high school students. The student's self-talk says, "I don't know anything about this" and is accompanied by an unwillingness to tackle the assigned work in his text and a visible disengagement from the rest of the class. Here is the ensuing dialogue between the student (S) and the teacher (T):

S: I really don't know anything about this.
T: Really? Let's look at what you don't know. Is it this whole chapter?
S: Well, uh, no, it's this section here.
T: This whole section?
S: Well, uh um, actually, it's this one part here that I don't understand. (Ackerman, 1997, personal communication)

The teacher then steps in to assist with the difficulty that the student himself has identified. When the teacher, Thad Ackerman, discussed his own intentions, he reported that he was aware, during the exchange, of wanting to be careful about "not denying the student's feelings of difficulty or discouragement." Caring listening means that the teacher accepts the student's own sense of things as the starting point. In this instance they also moved on to reach a more precise description. Ackerman told me he has observed that after a few of these exchanges, the students themselves begin to speak with more precision. This exchange exemplifies our conjunction of caring and honesty: the teacher practices caring listening, with no trace of being judgmental, while he simultaneously pursues the question of accuracy.

At this point one might object that models of teacher-student exchanges are fine, but we still have a transfer problem when we shift to self-talk. For example, how does one reconcile the emphasis on caring, nonjudgmental listening with the criterion of truth, or accuracy, especially when faced with the multiplicity of dubious distortions which sometimes run rampant through one's self-talk? A concern for accuracy seems to require us to be judgmental, at least about questions of honesty. If, however, we interpret being nonjudgmental (as I believe Noddings intends it) to mean that we are not preoccupied with questions of censure, or with the manufacture of justifications in order to defend against censure, then the framework of caring listening is that of a person who has a compassionate interest in understanding the truth of the situation, not of one who comes to pass judgment upon it.

If one sets aside the judgmental perspective, then the feeling that one has to "justify" the self gets undercut. Without the pressure for self-justification, it becomes easier to acknowledge all that might be "going on." I can, in a sense, listen to my own listening and hear what the whole clamoring mix of voices may be saying, even when they represent contradictory inclinations, embarrassing thoughts, or frightful feelings. A self-care approach with an emphasis on caring nonjudgmental inward listening can then support and enhance a commitment to internal honesty.

EDUCATING SELF-TALK

It is time now to look more closely at what practical connections we can make between our discussion so far and our original concern with the forms of self-care that lead a person to "choose for himself and not against himself . . . not only for his physical self but, more importantly, for his ethical self." (Noddings, 1984, p. 64) I believe that certain guidelines emerge out of our explorations thus far. We have seen that talk makes a suitable subject matter for ethical scrutiny and for the application of moral parameters (Ayim, 1997), which can in turn be applied not only to interpersonal communication but also to self-talk. Placed within the larger rubric of self-care, we noted that self-talk carries the potential to facilitate or hinder the development of an ethical self, even perhaps unbeknownst to the person himself or herself. Thus, it behooves us as educators to direct our students' conscious attention toward their covert self-talk voices.

To reach some degree of awareness about the nature and content of one's self-talk is in itself a major achievement for most people. This achievement may have the best chance of arising if one practices in an open, receptive, and nonjudgmental way. Teachers can model caring listening, explicitly structure opportunities for students to practice caring listening in reciprocal dialogues, and combine these with reflective discussions about how to undertake similar listening with self-talk.

Yet even if one does learn to do caring self-listening, this still may not be enough to protect and nourish the ethical self. For example, one might improve his or her ability to attend to self-talk only to become acutely aware of an ongoing barrage of self-loathing self-talk attacks. While such conscious awareness does seem a positive step beyond either suppression or denial, we still need to work with what gets discovered when someone does caring self-listening.

To learn to care for our ethical selves requires learning how to subject self-talk to ethical scrutiny. Such scrutiny could be pursued along the lines discussed earlier where one evokes criteria such as the Sufi "gates," the Buddhist constraints on "Right Speech," and/or Ayim's "good talk" parameters. The key is learning to discriminate between those self-talk discourses that support one's ethical self and those that do not.

The answer to our question of how to work with what gets discovered depends in large part upon the results of ethical scrutiny. If, for example, an instance of self-talk passes the tests of ethical scrutiny with flying colors, revealing itself as honest and ethically desirable, then encouragement, or what Noddings (1984, 1992) terms "confirmation," seems appropriate. If, however, the scrutiny reveals more mixed or predominantly unethical self-talk, we face further pedagogical questions, as well as potential moral difficulties.

How might one undertake the ethical education of self-talk, especially in those cases where we encounter unethical voices? To start with, let us make a rather obvious threefold classification for the results that are likely to emerge from subjecting one's self-talk to ethical scrutiny: (1) good, (2) mixed, and (3) bad. In the first classification, let us place those cases already mentioned above, where one's self-talk seems unequivocally "good," that is, caring, accurate, and supportive of the ethical self. The second classification encompasses those times when we hear a cacophony of inner voices that sound ethically discordant, rather like what Noddings (1992) describes as a person's "array of possible motives ranging from the gross and grubby to some that are acceptable or even admirable" (p. 25). The second group contains an intermingling set of self-talk mixed messages, where not all can pass the test of ethical scrutiny. The third classification is reserved for clearly unethical self-talk voices. Let us consider appropriate responses within each of these classifications.

In the first case, where the self-talk carries predominantly positive ethical weight, one can respond with what Noddings, following Martin Buber, terms "confirmation." In "confirmation" one "sees the best self . . . and works . . . to actualize that self" (Noddings, 1984, p. 64). To actualize the best self we put our "motivational displacement" to work on behalf of the ethical self. According to Noddings (1992), when "motivational displacement" occurs between people, it means that "our motive energy is flowing toward others and their projects. I receive what the other conveys, and I want to respond in a way that furthers the other's purpose or project" (p. 16). Now, I want to suggest that just such motivational displacement becomes the appropriate self-caring response when someone "hears" his or her own ethically positive self-talk, or morally desirable inner urges and voices. In this case it means directing one's "flow of motive energy" so as to reinforce the choices and internal voices that represent one's ethical self.

Such a smooth flow of listening and acting in favor of one's ethical self does not, however, happen automatically for most people. It is quite possible to falter between the initial sounds of an inner sympathetic moral voice arising and the ensuing appropriate action. One source of such effective resistance comes from those "other voices" representing the "gross and grubby" that often arise almost simultaneously with the "good ones."

Indeed, if we listen attentively for any length of time, we may conclude that the second classification where ethical and unethical inner voices intermingle and do battle represents the most common self-talk condition. Here is where the gap or space between the practice of open receptive caring listening and the practice of motivational displacement needs to be widened and sustained. This intermediate space where we pause between inner listening and any ensuing action is where the ethical criteria must enter in to distinguish those voices that do deserve "confirmation" from those that do not.

Learning to pause in this gap and to bring in ethical considerations seems a long-term, perhaps a lifetime, task. Yet to begin to do so seems essential for the ethical education of self-talk, no less than for other impulses. We learn to stop before we engage our personal engines in a particular flow of motive energy; and we listen to ourselves in order to consider what seems truly caring for our ethical selves. In time the more favorable ethical voices have a better chance to gain in ascendancy. Rather like internal fine tuning amid the static of competing inner voices we start to receive a clear consistent signal from our ethical self-talk channel.

In cases that fit our third classification, where unethical self-talk dominates inner speech, we no longer have the option to focus on confirmation of ethically acceptable voices, since these simply are not there at present. Staying in the gap between open receptivity and action seems even more imperative. The question then becomes what to do once one has come to a sustained halt within that space. The first challenge would seem to be not only to stop long enough to notice the unethical nature of our self-talk, but also to stay stopped even longer so we can forestall the possibility of motivational energy flowing into a concomitant harmful action.

Let us hypothesize for the moment that someone has succeeded in self-listening, in noticing his or her insistent unethical self-talk voices, and in refraining from entering upon any concomitant unethical actions, is there anything further to be said or done from an educational perspective? In some cases, perhaps not. If we can, by open listening, by ethical discernment, and by a non-negotiable refusal to act on their behalf, persuade unethical inner voices to quiet down and leave town of their own accord, then our self-talk may simply "change the subject" with no residue left.

On the other hand, my own experience has been that even when certain unethical inner voices are not permitted to influence my actions, they sometimes continue to sound off with a sort of low-grade frequency; or these voices may leave for a while only to come back later, repeating the same inner tape at a louder volume. How can education help someone learn to handle, to work with, these troublesome inner voices? I have found a number of strategies that fit within the parameters for ethical education and can be learned as practical methods. Of these, the alternatives that I find most valuable and viable are: Refute and Replace; Detach and Distance; and Investigate and Look Deeply. Let us consider each of these in turn.

Refute and Replace

In a Refute and Replace response, one confronts his or her own unethical self-talk and counters it with a suitable rebuttal. One also creates a new self-talk script to replace the harmful inner voices. Various versions of Refute and Replace are probably the most common recommended remedies for harmful self-talk in general. For example, cognitive psychologists advise us to catch ourselves in the act of distorted self-downing inner talk, to refute these self-descriptions and replace them with more accurate self-supporting statements.

To replace an unethical self-talk script with an ethical rewrite, one would aim to make what is said more caring, helpful, and honest, neither denying the existence of problems nor exaggerating their degree of difficulty. For example, let us look at one of Albert Ellis's (1988) colorful self-talk rewrites. Here Ellis is demonstrating a rebuttal and replacement script to be used when a person has failed to keep up with her or his expectations for steady progress and has "fallen back" into some problematic behavior pattern:

> [First] you told yourself something like, "I should not have fallen back! How awful and shameful to fall back! I'm a pretty incompetent person to let myself

do a foolish thing like that!" Then you felt depressed, guilty, self-hating. Now ... you have changed to ... "It was most unfortunate and unpleasant that I fell back but that is the nature of humans, including myself, to take two steps forward and one step backward. And sometimes two or three steps backward! I'm hardly an incompetent person to let myself do a foolish thing like that, but a fairly competent person who sometimes acts incompetently. And that is my nature, too!—to at times act foolishly. What a pain in the butt! But I can do better than that, I am sure, in the future; and get right back to the progress that I formerly made. Okay: back to the drawing board!" (p. 158)

Although Ellis's script may not appear to be about an "ethical" issue, from the perspective of an ethic of self-care I believe it contains multiple moral issues. Perhaps the most obvious one is that of truthfulness or honesty. Ellis takes an untrue distorted self-attack and rewrites it into a more accurate self-talk description of the situation. Even though it seems clear that being honest and accurate in one's self-talk stands as a vital ethical requirement for one who would be self-caring, to achieve this is neither easy nor straightforward. For instance, how can we learn to work more honestly with self-talk concerning our own feelings?

To be honest, most of us sometimes do feel "awful," "depressed," and "guilty" when we fail to meet our standards or expectations. Yet these "honest" feelings are not usually self-caring. Ellis's example demonstrates one answer to this dilemma. The answer is that as people begin to correct their self-talk, they get more accurate descriptions of their situations, as well as more realistic expectations. This honest accuracy lays the groundwork for distinguishing between appropriate feelings such as concern, caution, sadness, disappointment, irritation, remorse and regret, on the one hand, and inappropriate feelings such as over-concern, anxiety, panic, rage, horror, guilt, and depression, on the other hand. We can see this distinction at work when Ellis first describes the person who has "fallen back" as feeling (inappropriately) "awful and shameful" as well as "depressed, guilty, self-hating." Then, after correcting for accuracy, he shifts to the more appropriate feelings that say this is "most unfortunate and unpleasant." After this shift the self-downing feelings of self-hatred and guilt can be replaced by ones that, while still less than cheerful, are more workable and self-accepting.

In an ethic of self-care, our understanding of self-acceptance also has direct bearing on our construction of the ethical self. In this regard, Ellis's script for changing self-talk demonstrates another important distinction that can be too easily missed, namely the difference between self-acceptance and self-indulgence. It has been my experience that both students and teachers sometimes conflate self-acceptance and self-indulgence, believing that self-acceptance means that one can just lean back and indulge in whatever present weaknesses happen to be there. This mistaken con-flation can lead either to the indulgent use of self-acceptance as an excuse for non-effort, or to the strenuous view that people should not be self accepting because self-acceptance will stifle one's urge toward greater achievements.

Ellis's script makes it clear that acknowledging our human nature does entail accepting our tendencies "to at times act foolishly." Yet this impor-tant self-acceptance in no way precludes getting right "back to the draw-ing board!" Indeed, a realistic self-acceptance may well provide the best vantage point from which to select a propitious direction or timely course of action.

Detach and Distance

In some cases, after a little practice, we can succeed at replacing old scripts with new ones and learn to "talk ourselves out of" certain stuck debilitating inner tapes. In other cases, however, we discover that a great deal of our internal chatter continues to come and go with a life of its own. As DuPrau (1992), in her inimitable way, puts it: "We say, 'I'm thinking about such and such,' when really it would be more accurate to say, 'Thoughts about such and such are tearing through my head'" (p. 101). How does one find a self-caring response in those instances where chang-ing the current self-talk content remains a remote possibility?

The person has already "listened" many times to the same old repeti-tive thoughts that are once again "tearing through" his or her head. She or he has clearly determined that what's being said does not meet the cri-teria for Right Speech, or for Caring Speech, or for any form of ethically Good Talk. The student has attempted to apply the standard corrective remedies, such as refuting, rewriting, and replacing these internal scripts, and yet the uncaring self-attacks or self-disparagements continue more or less unabated. At this point, the strategy of Detach and Distance might be the best response.

To undertake a Detach-and-Distance response means to put as much psychological space as possible between unethical inner voices and one's sense of self, especially the self that controls one's flow of motive energy. Instead of engaging in rebuttals and refutations, one consciously chooses to disregard contentious inner messages and to ignore or attempt to marginalize these voices. Even though they may be clamoring for our at-tention, we do our best to give them as little attention as possible. We do not, however, deny their existence or pretend we do not hear these voices at all. The practice of Detach and Distance should not be confused with denial or repression.

The key to successful use of a Detach-and-Distance strategy lies in learning how to change one's relationship to the unethical self-talk. In a sense, one learns to practice caring toward his or her uncaring self-talk, rather than treating it as an adversary. This calls for an expansion of self-directed caring so as to include even one's own uncaring self-talk. Or to put it another way, the student needs to provide a spacious enough holding environment, where she or he does not resort to condemnation, denial, or repression, but neither does she or he allow for harmful effects toward anyone, oneself included. How might this be done? What would an example look like, feel like, sound like?

One of my favorite examples comes from Natalie Goldberg's book *Writing Down the Bones* (1986). Her brief essay entitled "Trouble with the Editor" demonstrates what I am calling the Detach-and-Distance strategy. But first we need to substitute our own inner characters for Goldberg's. For her "creator," let us read "ethical self"; and when Goldberg describes the self-attacking voices of her "editor or internal censor," imagine your own versions of self-attack inner voices. Keeping these substitutions in mind, here is Goldberg's (1986) advice:

> It is important to separate the creator and the editor or internal censor. . . . If the editor is absolutely annoying . . . sit down whenever you need to and write what the editor is saying; give it full voice—"You are a jerk, who ever said you could write, I hate your work, you suck, I'm embarrassed, you have nothing valuable to say, and besides, you can't spell. . . ." Sound familiar?
>
> The more clearly you know the editor, the better you can ignore it. After a while, like the jabbering of an old drunk fool, it becomes just prattle in the background. Don't reinforce its power by listening to its empty words. If the voice says, "You are boring," . . . hear "You are boring" as distant white laundry flapping in the breeze. Eventually it will dry up and someone miles away will fold it and take it in. Meanwhile you will continue to write. (p. 26)

How does this example illustrate a caring approach toward uncaring self-talk? To start with, Goldberg meets our criterion for open, receptive listening. Indeed, Goldberg goes so far as to suggest that one even take dictation, so to speak, to write down what the "internal censor" has to say, "give it full voice." Although writing down what an uncaring internal voice has to say may seem, at first glance, to be counterproductive, in practice this is often the most effective initial step students can take toward changing their relationship with persistent internal self-attacks. David Burns (1989), an experienced advocate for the practice of writing down upsetting thoughts and negative feelings, emphasizes the fact that "Once you get them down on paper, you develop a more objective perspective. . . . You will see in black and white just how unrealistic they are" (p. 73). In classrooms, once students start to write these down, they can then discuss their own worst forms of self-attack with other students. Sharing these becomes both reassuring and amusing. Furthermore, from an ethical perspective, it means that one not only sees "in black and white just how unrealistic they are," one also sees how judgmental, dishonest, unnecessary, unkind, unhelpful, untimely, uncaring, and hurtful they are.

In brief, listening to and writing down what their internal voices have to say, however uncaring, repetitious, and outrageous these sayings may be, gives students the chance to detach from the content and appraise it from a more accurate ethical perspective. Then, as Natalie Goldberg says, students may still hear these voices, but only as "just prattle in the background" or "as distant white laundry flapping in the breeze."

The last two sentences in Goldberg's example both carry significant points. Her final sentence: "Meanwhile you will continue to write" demonstrates the ability to sustain an effective gap between open, receptive listening to the "censor" and any concomitant change in one's flow of motive energy. From our perspective, students would learn how to "hear" inner voices and how to "stop and think" ethically so that unethical self-talk voices would remain just that—voices and no more, without any motive power to effect action.

An important corollary message that accompanies this point is contained in Goldberg's penultimate sentence: "Eventually it will dry up and someone miles away will fold it and take it in." This imagery aptly fits what is often a prolonged process. The diminishment of internal uncaring voices tends to be a slow, gradual, eventual fading out, rather than a quick fix. Most students will have to practice with considerable conscious awareness before they manage to put "miles" of space between their most persistent self-attack themes and their ethical selves.

In addition, I find Goldberg's allusion to "someone miles away" to be a telling reference. First, it conveys the way we can detach our personal identification from such voices and can create a real sense of distance comparable to their being "miles away." Second, it reminds me of another form of "distance," namely, that the original sources for some of our most habitual tenacious inner self-attacks come from someone else "miles away" such as parents, siblings, or other ancient significant others. And this is one reason why we may need to go to our third form of response, which asks us to Investigate and Look Deeply.

Investigate and Look Deeply

To Investigate and Look Deeply means to me to proceed above all in a spirit of inquiry. Although in certain cases one might require or want to resort to therapeutic forms of inquiry, there are many avenues for educational inquiry as well. We may, for example, discover common cultural sources and societal practices that promote unethical self-talk patterns. These might be identified, studied, and queried. The salient point is that students can learn the methods and acquire the skills needed to use any of our approaches as tools for ethical inquiry. What might this entail in the arena of Investigate and Look Deeply?

First of all, we do not want to abandon our initial commitment to caring listening. Without caring listening toward unethical self-talk, one runs the dangers of repression, mystification, and projection. Caring listening, coupled with attention to honesty, helpfulness, and timeliness, thus seem to be crucial practices but insufficient conditions for undertaking what Noddings (1989) calls "Educating for a Morality of Evil" (chapter 9), where we must question and investigate "the power of mystification and repression" (p. 229). As Noddings says, "evil is real, and to control it we need to understand it and accept that the tendency toward it dwells in all of us" (pp. 229–230).

Thus in situations where unethical self-talk and the potential for moral evil predominate, additional criteria, or aims, for the ethical education of self-talk are required. These would seem to include (1) a discerning awareness that can identify, or recognize, unethical internal voices, dubious motives, or hurtful impulses, as such; (2) a willingness to acknowledge these as part of one's own indwelling tendencies; (3) an ability to control harmful impulses, so that one is able to refrain from acting upon the dictates of unethical self-talk; and (4) a commitment to moral self-inquiry that searches for understanding when unethical self-talk arises.

Our expanding list of criteria may now seem to have created such a complex task that it could appear overwhelming. But to put this into practice is much more commonplace than the complexity of our analysis might suggest. Let us look at an example of how one 14-year-old practices caring self-listening and applies the criteria for ethical discernment to his own self-talk. The following example comes from Thich Nhat Hanh (1991), who describes the experiences of a boy who studied with him at Plum Village (a mindfulness retreat center in France). Here is his account:

A fourteen-year-old boy who practices at Plum Village told me this story. When he was eleven, he was very angry at his father. Every time he fell down and hurt himself, his father would shout at him. The boy vowed to himself that when he grew up, he would be different. But last year, his little sister was playing with other children and she fell off a swing and scraped her knee. It was bleeding, and the boy became very angry. He wanted to shout at her, "How stupid! Why did you do that?" But he caught himself. Because he had practiced breathing and mindfulness, he could recognize his anger and he did not act on it.

The adults were taking good care of his sister, washing her wound and putting a Band-Aid on it, so he walked away slowly and practiced breathing on his anger. Suddenly he saw that he was exactly like his father. He told me, "I realized that if I didn't do something about the anger in me, I would transmit it to my children." At the same time, he saw something else. He saw that his father may have been a victim just like him. The seeds of his father's anger might have been transmitted by his grandparents. (pp. 71–72)

This example illustrates a number of pertinent points. First, it is interesting to note that the boy's account of his initial motivation for his "vow" not to shout at others when they are hurt matches up with Rousseau's alignment between children's sense of their own rights and their capacity to respond sympathetically toward others. The boy's stated determination to act differently reflects both the sense that he deserved better treatment from his father and also the feeling that he envisioned himself acting in a more compassionate, sympathetic way toward others.

Second, the way the boy "vowed to himself that when he grew up he would be different" shows a certain conscious construction of his own ethical ideal akin to that advocated by Noddings. Of further significance is the method he uses for constructing the ethical ideal; by vowing to himself that "he would be different," the boy relies on the use of positive self-talk. And we can see its efficacy in enabling him to pause in the gap between his awareness of the impulse to shout at his sister and the actual execution of that shout. Within Noddings' framework we can say that he has "received" these internal voices, which echo his father's responses, but he has paused long enough to make a clear ethical choice not to give their "project" the energy of "motivational displacement." The boy manages to stop himself before he says anything out loud that might be hurtful or unfair to his sister.

Thus, the boy's ethical ideal has already begun to function for him alongside the still extant impulses for an unethical conditioned reaction (in this case, anger and shouting). Indeed, there is a close resemblance to what Noddings (1984) advocates when she writes:

Nothing is more important in nurturing the ethical ideal than attribution and explication of the best possible motive. The one-caring holds out to the child a vision of his lovely self actualized or nearly actualized. . . . He does not have to reject and castigate himself, but he is encouraged to move toward an ideal that is, in an important sense, already real in the eyes of a significant other. (p. 123)

In the case of self-talk, each person becomes his or her own "significant other" and makes the ethical ideal "already real in the eyes of" his or her own parallel self-consciousness. At the same time one does not deny that "evil is real, and to control it we need to understand it and accept that the tendency toward it dwells in all of us" (Noddings, 1989, pp. 229–230). The boy in Thich Nhat Hanh's example does accept this tendency and he seeks to understand it, thus discovering the connections to social conditioning.

In conclusion, we can say that this 14-year-old boy appears to have met our full listing of criteria. He acts according to the ethical ideal, caring for his sister by stopping himself before he shouts at her, caring for himself by walking away slowly, breathing mindfully, and caring for the angry voices that emerge in his self-talk by keeping his consciousness open to them. In looking deeply, the boy finds not only a measure of understanding concerning the tendencies toward anger that dwell in all of us, but also a more sympathetic understanding toward his father. He reaches a "true affection of the heart enlightened by reason"; and he makes a clear choice for and not against his ethical self.

Acknowledgments. I wish to thank Michael Andrew, Susan D. Franzosa, Barbara Houston, Michael Katz, Jane Roland Martin, Beatrice Nelson, Nel Noddings, Joe Onosko, Jennifer Radden, and Janet Farrell Smith for their helpful responses to earlier drafts of this chapter.

REFERENCES

Ayim, Maryann. (1997). *The moral parameters of good talk.* Waterloo, Ontario, Canada: Wilfrid Laurier University Press.

Burns, David. (1989). *The feeling good handbook.* New York: Penguin.

DuPrau, Jeanne. (1992). *The earth house.* New York: Fawcett Columbine.

Ellis, Albert. (1988). *How to stubbornly refuse to make yourself miserable about anything—yes, anything!* New York: Lyle Stuart.

Gendlin, Eugene. (1981). *Focusing.* New York: Bantam Books.

Goldberg, Natalie. (1986). *Writing down the bones.* Boston: Shambala.

Hanh, Thich Nhat. (1991). *Peace is every step.* New York: Bantam Books.

Houston, B. (1993). Speaking candidly. In Audrey Thompson (Ed.), *Philosophy of education 1993* (pp. 110–113). Urbana, IL: Philosophy of Education Society.

Kornfield, Jack. (Ed.). (1993). *Teachings of the Buddha.* Boston: Shambala.

Noddings, Nel. (1984). *Caring: A feminine approach to ethics and moral education.* Berkeley: University of California Press.

Noddings, Nel. (1989). *Women and evil.* Berkeley: University of California Press.

Noddings, Nel. (1992). *The challenge to care in schools.* New York: Teachers College Press.

Rousseau, Jean-Jacques. (1911). *Émile* (Barbara Foxley, Trans.). New York: Dutton, Everyman's Library. (Original work published 1762)

CHAPTER 6

Caring, Justice, and Self-Knowledge

William L. Blizek

When I was asked to write a chapter for this book, I was delighted to have the opportunity to say some of the things about caring and justice that are not said clearly enough or often enough in the philosophical literature. As I thought about what I wanted to say, however, it struck me that although my ideas might be interesting to philosophers, they would make little, if any, difference in the lives of classroom teachers who want to be more fair and caring persons and who want to promote fairness and caring in their students. I decided to focus, therefore, on what I believe to be a key ingredient in acting fairly and caring for others, namely, self-knowledge.

Whatever our theories about the nature of caring or fairness may be, it is always possible that we may misapply these theories in specific cases if we are unaware of our own motivation. From the theoretical perspective, we have sufficient knowledge to treat others fairly or with care. We know in many cases what it takes to treat someone fairly, or we often know that particular behaviors are uncaring. Yet we are not able or are unwilling to treat others fairly or with care. We regularly deceive ourselves about what we are doing. Sorting out theoretical technicalities, then, will not contribute as much to our moral behavior as will greater self-awareness.

In the following essay I would like to reiterate some of the ideas about caring and fairness that I think are especially important. These ideas are, I believe, available in our culture to such an extent that every teacher will have run across them at one time or another, in one form or another. Having identified these ideas, I then will identify some of the areas in which a lack of self-knowledge affects how we treat our students and how we influence the behavior of those students.

RELATIONSHIP BETWEEN CARING AND FAIRNESS

Before turning to some of the basic ideas about caring and fairness found in our culture, let me say just a word about the relationship between caring and fairness. There are, I believe, a variety of views on the nature of caring and the nature of fairness. Depending upon which views one adopts, one may see caring as incompatible with fairness (or vice versa), or one may see unfair behavior as also uncaring (and vice versa).

A department chair was asked, for example, to apply a strict set of guidelines for determining merit pay increases. After the guidelines had been strictly applied, however, it turned out that one member of the department, through no fault of her own, was significantly disadvantaged. The chair then modified the strict application of the guidelines so as to no longer disadvantage this particular faculty member. The chair did this as a matter of caring for the faculty member—alleviating considerable suffering and embarrassment—but the modification changed the outcome of the merit pay process such that everyone else got less than they would have had the guidelines been strictly applied. The other faculty were treated unfairly—at least, in one sense of fairness—in order to prevent significant harm to one member of the department. In this case, caring took precedence over fairness. They were incompatible because the chair could not treat the other faculty fairly and care for the individual disadvantaged by the strict application of merit pay guidelines.

We may reinterpret this example, however, to show that the important difference is one between procedural justice and substantive justice. That is, the procedure designed to bring about a fair result actually failed to do so in the case of one faculty member. That individual did not in any way deserve the harm that came to her from the strict application of the guidelines. We might say, then, that caring for individual X is incompatible with various procedures for achieving fairness, but that caring for individual X is also a matter of treating X fairly in the substantive sense. Even if caring were always compatible with substantive justice, however, caring will sometimes be incompatible with procedural justice. Since we are a culture consumed by concern for procedural justice, especially in education, we will need to be aware of these possible conflicts.

From a different perspective, we might say that when we treat someone unfairly we are not caring for them, or that when we are not caring for them we are treating them unfairly, not giving them what they deserve.

Some faculty give other faculty very low scores on the merit pay scale, scores that are obviously contrary to the evidence. I believe that these scores are given as a matter of spite. My guess is that similar situations on college campuses across the country are rather common. These situations might involve votes on summer teaching, leaves of absence, tenure, or promotion, rather than votes on merit pay, but having faculty vote to reward a friend or punish a perceived enemy seems to be a common occurrence. In such cases, those receiving the low scores or negative votes were not treated fairly, nor were they treated with care. There is no reason to believe that uncaring and unfairness cannot go hand in hand.

Given this discussion, it seems to me that we do not have general principles of fairness or caring which tell us exactly what to do in each particular case. Each situation will have different factors that determine the outcome as much as the general ideas of fairness or caring. This means that there is much more room for judgment in our moral decision making than if general principles gave us precise answers in all situations.

We might adopt more specific rules, of course, and apply these without taking differences between situations into account, but this strict application of rules often seems to yield unsatisfactory results, results that seem unfair or uncaring in some other sense of those terms, and we will have to use our judgment to decide when the strict application is acceptable and when it does not yield satisfactory results. (For a discussion of the difference between principles and rules, see "The Model of Rules I" in Dworkin, 1977, pp. 14–45.) In either case, whether we apply general principles or specific rules, judgment will come into play in our moral deliberations. But giving judgment more weight than the strict application of rules opens the door to the kind of self-deception that enables us to claim or think that we are acting fairly or with care, when in fact we are not doing so.

IMPORTANCE OF ATTITUDES TO CARING

Let me now identify some of the ideas to be found in our popular culture that enable us to think clearly about justice, caring, and self-knowledge. Some of these ideas have identifiable sources and others just seem to float through the culture in one form or another with some frequency.

Influencing Self-Esteem

One idea that is popular these days is self-esteem. We all realize that it is important for individuals to value themselves, but we also realize that being valued by others is an important part of valuing ourselves. If no one else finds us valuable, it is particularly difficult to find ourselves to be valuable. And, on those occasions when someone else indicates that we are not valuable or important, we find these occasions to be very hurtful.

To put this another way, the attitude of others toward us (finding us valuable or not valuable) is an important part of our lives. It is not just what people do to us or for us that matters, but how they do it, or with what attitude they do what they do. The attitudes that others have toward us have consequences—they generate happiness or pain—and these consequences are as important to us as any of the other consequences of the actions of others.

Actually, I think that the consequences of the attitudes of others toward us are often overlooked in the philosophical discussion of right and wrong action. They are overlooked because attitudes are not as easy to recognize as some of the more obvious consequences of our actions. The attitude of the other is often conveyed by the look in his or her eye, the tone of his voice, or her body language—as opposed to, for example, the lending of the money or the keeping of the promise. Attitudes are, nevertheless, an important part of our understanding of how to treat others and how we ourselves want to be treated.

While the attitudes of others may be described in a variety of ways, I think that the most important distinction is between viewing someone as an equal or as less valuable than oneself. In the history of bad human behavior, human beings seem to be able to treat other human beings terribly only when they see other human beings as less than themselves (or see others as not really human). To me this suggests that anytime I encounter someone who sees me as less important or valuable than himself or herself, I am threatened. I feel fear in relation to the other, because I know that the other is *willing* to treat me badly—even if he or she does not actually treat me badly.

In view of this analysis, it does not seem foolish to say that the attitude of the other may be more important, at least in some cases, than what the other person does. I need to borrow some money to help pay my daughter's college expenses. I am sure that my father will lend me the money (at a lower interest rate than the bank). When my father lends me the money, however, it comes with a lecture about how I should handle my finances differently from the way that I do. But it is not just that I should behave differently (this might well be true), it is the message that I am a disappointment to my father, that I am less than what my father wants me to be, that I am, at least in this arena, less valuable than my father, that is troublesome and hurtful. My father's attitude is so hurtful to me that I am willing to borrow the money from the bank and pay the higher interest rather than suffer being told again how I am less valuable than my father because I have not done what he did and what he told me to do. Yes, my father will lend me the money. But the pain I feel because of his attitude toward me makes the receiving of the money so problematic that I will look elsewhere for the loan.

Talk about self-esteem seems to be a prevalent part of our popular culture. I have tried to describe the self-esteem talk in terms of attitudes and the consequences of attitudes because this fits with what I take to be an important part of caring. Caring is not just a matter of doing something, of acting in a particular way. It is also a matter of attitude. Caring is a matter of doing the right thing, but it is also a matter of doing it, to paraphrase Aristotle, "to the right person, to the right extent, at the right time, with the right attitude, and in the right way." (McKeon, 1941, p. 963.)

Doing the same thing with the wrong attitude introduces fear or the pain of being disvalued into the situation. We are then treated as less valuable than the other or as an object to be manipulated by the other, and when we are so treated, we are not treated with care. The wrong attitude changes what could be a caring act into one that is uncaring.

Understanding Motivation

Another way of talking about the attitude of others and its importance to the moral nature of our interactions is to talk in terms of what motivates the other. Is the motivation my best interest, or is the motivation some benefit to the other? I ask my friend Bob to help me move some furniture over the weekend. He agrees to help me, but without telling me, he expects me to help him fix his car the following weekend. I do not realize what Bob's motivation is, until he asks me to help him with his car, and I say "no." Then Bob says to me, "But I helped you with moving furniture last weekend—now you owe me a similar amount of time and energy." Once I know that I owe Bob something, I realize that Bob's help with the furniture was not motivated merely by my best interests, but by Bob's need to fix his car—without taking it to the garage and paying a mechanic.

All of us can find similar examples. On some occasions we know at the very moment that someone has a "hidden agenda" or that there are "strings attached" to someone's offer to help. On other occasions we do not discover the real motive until later. Nevertheless, we all are familiar with interactions of this sort.

I do not believe that we can determine the motives of others in every case. And I believe that there are an infinite number of ways in which we can determine the motives of others. In one case it will be the tone of voice, in another it will be something the other says, and in yet another it will be something the other does. The particular circumstances will determine what method we use to understand the motives of another person. Nevertheless, we often do know what motivates someone else. At least we know when someone is motivated by our interests rather than their own.

The talk of hidden agendas and motives, strings attached, and so on is one of the ways we talk in this culture about what it means to care for another. We care for someone when there is no hidden agenda or motive behind the way in which we treat him or her. We care for someone when we act without attaching any strings to our action. We fail to care for someone when the real motive behind our action is some benefit to ourselves, rather than the interests of the other.

Talking About Interactions

Let me identify three other ways of talking about how we experience our interactions with others. The first of these is in terms of "selfishness" and "unselfishness." ("Altruism" and "egoism" are also terms which are used in this discussion.) We frequently notice when someone has acted in a way that seems to us to be unselfish. We value such behavior highly, even if it is not directed toward us. We value such behavior, I believe, for the reasons already discussed. What we describe as unselfish behavior is behavior that carries with it an attitude of equality, and therefore there is no threat from the other. When we describe behavior as selfish, we know that our interests will not be given equal consideration with those of the other and so we feel unequal, disvalued, and, at least to some extent, threatened. The more selfish behavior we experience in the world, the more threatening the world becomes.

The second way of talking about our interactions with others is in terms of being valued or feeling disvalued. I am standing with a group of men at a social gathering. The topics of conversation are only those topics of interest to the dominant speakers. If someone else introduces a new topic, it is ignored in favor of the "important" topics. Almost no opportunity to speak is given to those who are not the dominant speakers. How do the non-speakers feel? Disvalued. It is clear that the dominant speakers do not care what the non-speakers think or what they might contribute to the conversation. I might enjoy listening to the conversation, but I would not say that I feel valued, in the way that I feel valued when someone asks me what I think about the topic of conversation.

Finally, we also talk about being loved or not loved. The biblical admonition is to "love your neighbor as yourself" (Mark 12:31). We are told that if we do something to the "least of these my brethren," we are treating them as though they were Jesus (Matthew 25:40). We are taught to "do unto others as you would have them do unto you" (Matthew 7:12), or to "not do unto others as you would not want them to do to you." In all of these cases, it seems to me that we are talking about the attitude we have toward others.

We may dispute the theoretical implications of the examples I have given above, but what I have tried to do is to show that such language is used regularly in our culture. And as a matter of practice, people use this language and understand it to the extent that they can avoid or seek out particular kinds of interactions. If you say to someone, "I think there are strings attached to the arrangements you are making," that person knows exactly what you mean and that the situation must be approached with caution, even if they do not know exactly what the "strings" are. If someone says to me that Bob is helping me for his own reasons and not just because he wants to help me, I, too, know what this means and I adjust my response to Bob accordingly.

All of this language and these ideas may be troublesome theoretically, but as a matter of practice, we use this language and these ideas with ease, and our use of them plays an important part in the way we live our lives. Indeed, the term *care* may be a more recent addition to our moral vocabulary, one that has received considerable attention since the publication of Carol Gilligan's *In a Different Voice* (1982; see also Nel Noddings, 1984). The ideas associated with caring, however, seem to be a regular part of our discussion of human behavior, especially the ideas that motive or attitude are an important element in how we treat others and in how we experience being treated by others.

SUBSTANTIVE JUSTICE

Before turning to some examples of how the lack of self-knowledge or self-deception affects our behavior, let me say a word or two about the concept of justice. I have already said something about the difference between procedural and substantive justice, so here I will try to draw a distinction between two views of substantive justice.

One view, taken from John Rawls (1971), is that the qualities we have as a result of the natural lottery should not determine our place in the social and economic order. We should all be treated equally, unless we are doing something that benefits the least advantaged of society. It is on this view that teachers should be paid more than movie stars because teachers make a much more significant contribution to the least advantaged.

The other view is taken from Robert Nozick (1974). On this view, our holdings are fairly ours as long as they have been transferred to us freely by someone else who held it fairly. We deserve what others are willing to give us. Although Nozick's view is more complicated than I have described, it is, in essence, a free market view on which movie stars deserve more than teachers because more people freely transfer their wealth to the movie stars (by freely buying tickets to their movies) than they do to teachers (by voting for school board members who promise not to raise property taxes).

While these two views of justice are often seen as incompatible, it seems to me that they each capture something that we ordinarily think is important in how we treat others. We do think both that movie stars deserve their greater wealth because it has been given freely to them *and* that teachers should earn more than movie stars because the contribution that they make to our lives is so much greater than the contribution of movie stars.

The result of this seeming conflict is, I believe, that each view of justice captures something important to us and that in some contexts one view of justice will be more appropriate than the other and vice versa. Neither view by itself will give us an adequate account of justice. We need both—sometimes one and sometimes the other. Here again, the fact that we must decide which contexts call for which notion of justice leaves us relying on our judgment, rather than on rules or deduction or simple calculation. As long as our judgment determines which view of justice is important, then, we must be sure that our judgment is not determined by self-deception.

AREAS OF SELF-DECEPTION

I would now like to provide some examples of ways in which we as teachers deceive ourselves about our motivations in interacting with our students and with others. The examples that I provide are taken from my own experience or experiences that others have shared with me. The experiences of each reader, however, may be quite different from mine. I hope that my examples, however, will lead the reader to reflect upon his or her own experiences and that in that reflection he or she will find his or her own examples of self-deception. The first step is to recognize cases in which self-deception enters into moral deliberations, into discussions of caring or fairness. Since it often is easier to recognize others' self-deception than one's own, this is a good place to start. Listen carefully to how others talk about the issues. The most important step, however, is to discover where our own lack of self-knowledge, our own self-deception, enters into the discussion of caring and fairness that we ourselves carry out.

I have selected four areas where I think that we are likely or more likely to deceive ourselves about our motivation or attitude than other areas. These areas are status, power, sexuality, and religion. I discuss each of these areas in different ways. Since there are so many possibilities, my hope is that some of the examples in each section will resonate with the reader, that is, resonate sufficiently so that the reader will find my general claims about the importance of self-knowledge convincing.

Status

It seems to me that one of the things that strongly motivates all of us, teachers included, is status, or, at least, the perception of status. In education I believe that we frequently use students to increase or enhance our own personal status. But this is not what we identify as our motivation. We give all kinds of justifications for our behavior, our too frequently bad behavior, but we do not admit to being motivated by our own status.

In higher education, faculty have greater status, roughly speaking, if they advise more theses and dissertations. The reason may be that students select faculty with greater status, hoping that the status of the faculty will rub off on the student, or that some faculty are better advisors than others. In either case you can imagine my making dishonest, misleading, or disparaging remarks about another faculty member in an effort to have a student select me for his or her thesis advisor.

In such a case, I have not acted fairly, in the case of either the student or the other faculty member. In this case, acting unfairly is also an example of acting without care—I am not acting to promote the best interests of my student, although that is what I would claim to both myself and others, but rather to promote my own status. It might well be that it would be better, all things considered, for the student to have another faculty member as an advisor, but I have denied the student what is best in order to have another advisee.

Another example is the curriculum. Do we select a Discipline-Based Art Education curriculum because it is in the best interests of our students or because then we can say that we are adopting a cutting-edge curriculum or because we might be able to get a grant to prepare the new courses? Do we argue for a course on the philosophy of language because it will benefit large numbers of students or because we would like our curriculum to look as much as possible like the curriculum of the school from which we graduated? Do we vote against changing the curriculum for our fourth grade class because it will not benefit the students or because it will require a great deal of time and effort on the part of the teacher? It seems to me that many curricular decisions are better described as efforts to increase faculty status or to serve faculty interests than as efforts to provide the best possible educational opportunities. Such decisions are neither fair nor are they decisions based on care.

Consider the case of "professor-as-guru." The guru behaves in ways that attract a loyal band of admirers. The status sought here is not status in one's profession or even status among one's peers, but rather the status given by a select group of students or former students. The important thing for the guru is to be very much admired (one might say, adored) by a small group of students. But all of this behavior is done in the name of providing special educational opportunities. And what is the result? One guru I know of gives his loyal students special opportunities, but these same students spend considerable time running errands and doing other menial work that is beneficial to the productivity of the guru but is not beneficial to the students. Another guru finds adoring female students easier targets for sexual conquest. In both cases students are treated unfairly—should a student have to run errands to get a glowing letter of recommendation?—and without care, without concern for their best interests.

The examples above have concerned the relationship between teachers and students. But the need for status by teachers also can affect their relationship with school staff. How frequently does the need for status lead a teacher to speak to someone on the staff in a tone of voice meant to indicate that the teacher is more important than the staff member? For some time a friend of mine worked as the secretary of an academic department. Every teacher in the department liked her very much. Yet with great frequency they would interact with her in a way that indicated that they were more important. Some would badger, some would wheedle, and others would flatter, but there was no equality in the interaction, and my friend experienced considerable pain from being treated this way. Maybe it was more painful because faculty who would treat her ordinarily as an equal or as an important member of the team would treat her, on some occasions, with contempt: "I don't like to pull rank, but. . . ." I am confident that wherever you teach you will have experienced teacher/staff interactions in which the teacher treats staff members as though they are inferior. Such behavior/attitude is neither fair nor caring.

Finally, I want to consider the attitude that many faculty have toward those who are not as intelligent as they are. Usually one needs a significant level of academic intelligence—what Howard Gardner (1993) identifies as linguistic intelligence and logical-mathematical intelligence—to be a member of a university faculty. Having academic intelligence sets faculty apart from others, even if others have high levels of different kinds of intelligence (for example, spatial intelligence, bodily-kinesthetic intelligence, or interpersonal intelligence). Having academic intelligence makes us special. It gives us value. We have something that many others do not have, and we have higher levels of an intelligence that is highly valued in our culture.

The problem here is that different people have different levels of academic intelligence, and these differences can turn into differences in value. That is, faculty may feel that those with lower levels of academic intelligence are inferior as persons, even when those with low levels of academic intelligence may have high levels of other intelligences. I am confident that you have heard faculty talk about how dumb students are or about how many dumb students they have or even about how dumb members of the staff and administration can be. (For an interesting discussion of what it does and does not mean to be "smart," see Astin, 1997.)

What I envision is something like this. Many students in colleges and universities have less academic intelligence than does the faculty. The faculty then treats those students as generally inferior (rather than simply intellectually inferior). That treatment takes many forms: the tone of our voices; our refusal to spend the same amount of time with average students as we do with our best students; the things we say about our students—for example, our students only want to get a better job or they only want to participate in the social life of the campus. They are not like us. You can hear similar derision when faculty talk about other career opportunities.

Do our students deserve to be thought of and treated as generally inferior to us just because they have less academic intelligence or even less interest in academic matters than we have? How painful is it for our students to be treated as inferiors? Similarly, how painful it is for others in the university to be treated as inferiors? Surely we cannot be said to be caring for those students and others toward whom we have adopted an attitude of what I would describe as intellectual snobbery.

Power

I now turn to the issue of power. Power is often recognized by a pattern of behavior rather than by the outward behavior of a single instance. Suppose, for example, that a member of the thesis committee upon which I am serving asks that several small changes be made in the thesis before it is finally approved. This request might be made politely, and although the changes seem minor to me, I do not think much more of the request. Someone else on the committee, however, may recognize that this is something that the other member of the committee does on every committee on which he or she serves. And when someone once suggested to the other that the changes were not worth the effort, the response was, "I won't be able to sign off until the changes are made." The pattern of behavior here or the clues from several committees suggest that this is an individual who wishes to exercise power in the thesis process, and since the changes are not important, it appears to be only the power that is important to the individual. There is nothing unfair in the faculty's behavior, at least in one sense of fairness, but his or her behavior can be seen as uncaring.

Imagine a faculty meeting where some item of business is being discussed. The discussion does not seem to be going well or, at any rate, going forward. It occurs to me in situations like this that there is often some kind of hidden agenda that is driving the discussion. When we are not able to arrive at our conclusions as a matter of reason, there is usually something else at work, and often this is a question of power. Some faculty want one outcome, and others want another outcome. Reason leads us to one or the other of these outcomes (or even to a third alternative), but the discussion is not moving toward this outcome. Now it is a question of power. Which side will win? Various maneuvers come into play by both sides and the battle is on. One side may eventually win the struggle, and while the winners may feel good about their exercise of power, one of the negative aspects of such conflict is that it does not engender cooperative relationships between the parties involved. In a situation such as this I may be on the winning side—I have exercised power—but the result may be that my colleagues are left with hurt feelings. Or the losers may recognize that the winners were more concerned about winning than about the results of the outcome, results that, for example, might be unfair to students or to an individual faculty member.

Power is also an important ingredient in teacher/student interactions. Surely we sometimes *insist* that things will be our way because the student simply is not listening to the reasons for our decision. Students can be as manipulative as anyone else. But on some occasions a teacher will insist that things be done his or her way (the rules permit it) even when colleagues are unable to understand the reasoning given. In such cases the exercise of power seems to me to be more important than treating the student with care or treating the student fairly.

One of the arenas of power that has received considerable attention over the past several years is that of sexual harassment. Sometimes people respond to accounts of sexual harassment by saying, "Why doesn't he (or she) find his sexual satisfaction at home with his spouse or in an adult relationship with an equal?" But the answer is that it is not the usual sexual satisfaction that the harasser is after. The harasser is intent on making or forcing the other to do something that he or she does not want to do, something sexual in nature in the case of sexual harassment. It is the exer-

cise of power that brings satisfaction to the harasser, and this is one reason why the harasser is likely to pick someone vulnerable to be his victim—because it is easier to exercise power over the weak than over the
strong.

Sexuality

I now want to talk about sexuality as a motive for interacting with
others, whether they be students, faculty, or staff. I believe that we often
interact with others in order to satisfy our sexual desires and frequently
we do this without recognizing it or at the same time that we give other
reasons for our interactions. These interactions, insofar as they remain
unacknowledged, are sometimes damaging to others or unfair to others.
Suppose, for example, that I spend so much time with a student I find
sexually attractive that I do not have time to spend with other students
(male or female). In this case, it seems to me that I am treating other students unfairly. I will claim, of course, that I am just helping an interested
student—"She might become a philosophy major." But the real motivation
is satisfying my sexual desire to be in the presence of a sexually stimulat-
ing other.

I should make it clear here that I am not talking about the usual instances of sexual interaction between teachers and students. I am not talking about teachers who "have sex" with their students. I mean to be talking about something that is far more subtle. I believe that all of us (both
men and women) find others to be sexually attractive and that we enjoy
being in the presence of others we find sexually attractive. I do not mean
that someone is sexually attractive by meeting some standard of sexual
attractiveness that applies to everyone. Someone may be sexually attractive to me, but not to others. Yet that sexual attraction may be the moti-
vating factor in much of my behavior, behavior that may be both uncaring and unfair to the one I find sexually attractive, or uncaring and unfair
to others.

Since sexuality is such a taboo subject in our culture (even if crude
sexuality is displayed in advertisements, on television, and in movies), I
think that we do not pay much attention to this element of our sexuality.
That is, we do not pay much attention to our desire to be in the presence
of others whom we find sexually attractive. Nevertheless, I believe that these
desires play a much larger role in our interactions with others than we are
willing to admit or even consider. And if we are not aware of these desires
we may treat others badly when we think that we have good reasons for
treating them in the way that we do. Not all such sexual interactions need
to be damaging—especially when they are acknowledged. But when they

are not even considered, we are likely to find them pushing or pulling us in ways that cause us to treat others unfairly or without care.

Religion

Finally, I want to explore briefly the area of religion. I take up this issue because I find it to be an area where I may very well be deceiving myself. When I encounter particular "religious" responses from my students, I find myself getting angry. I feel the hair on the back of my neck stand up, and I feel my face flushing. I might not have paid much attention to this, but one of my students, a student whom I liked and respected, pointed it out to me. When I am angry, I am likely to speak to the student in a tone of voice that suggests inferiority, not only to myself, but also to other students. Students who are spoken to in this way feel the kind of pain that I described above, so I am not treating them with care, and they are less likely to participate in the class, thus increasing the likelihood that they are being treated unfairly.

The kind of religious response that bothers me is one where a commonplace religious explanation is given for something that occurs. A student might say something like, "Oh, that bad thing happened because it is God's will." Or a student might say that someone's suffering is a result of his or her sin. Or that the way to be a good person is to let the *Lord* into our lives. There are many similar phrases, but I will assume that you are familiar with this way of talking about the world.

Now, one way to respond is to criticize the answer as thoughtless. I could say simply that such answers are unacceptable, because they do not indicate a process of thinking about the questions or issue, and such a claim would carry considerable weight or find wide acceptance in the university, where the very purpose of the institution is to encourage thoughtfulness. I might even see my anger as a kind of righteous indignation, directed not at the particular student, but rather directed at ignorance in general. Unfortunately, these explanations do not feel satisfying. I do not feel enlightened when such explanations are given. I do not feel relieved that the question of what is bothering me has been answered.

So, what is bothering me? I do not yet know (with complete certainty), but I do have some suspicions. I grew up in a religious home where I adopted the same kinds of beliefs that make me angry when my students share these beliefs with me. As I remember my past, I did think a great deal about these issues, but I thought about them only within the larger framework of my beliefs. Some answers or ideas I simply had to accept because those were the answers or ideas that my religion provided. But now I have come to see these same answers and ideas as self-serving and not ideas that indicate a caring for others, even though much of the talk was about caring for others. There are, I believe, two results. First, I feel betrayed by those who claimed to be caring for me. That is, I now see their response to me as serving to promote their religious views and not as serving my particular needs. Second, I feel guilty that I, too, claimed to care for others, when in fact I was simply serving my own needs.

I do not know how all of this will be resolved in the end, but I do now believe that the anger I feel when a student gives a religious response is an anger directed toward me or my past, and not toward the student. I still feel my face flush, my body become tense, and the hair on the back of my neck stand on end, but I now take some time to relax and to remind myself of the problem before I respond to the student. I then may ask why the student holds those views or I may move on to some other possible answers, but I do not direct my anger in the same way that I used to direct it at the student. I cannot guarantee that the student is now comfortable—he or she may see me flush or notice the change in my body language—but I believe that the damage I do as a teacher is less and that I have something to consider further if I want to eliminate the discomfort of my student altogether. (I do not believe that students should always feel comfortable in the classroom, but I do not believe that their discomfort should be caused by my anger.)

I have used the issue of religion in describing my own lack of self-knowledge and the harm that such a lack of knowledge may cause my students because this is the arena of self-knowledge that has become important to me recently. A lack of self-knowledge about one's relationship to religion may not be of concern to others, but there are probably different arenas which generate for others similar behavior in relation to students, behavior that is neither fair nor caring, behavior which does not encourage either fairness or caring in the classroom.

CONCLUSION

In the preceding essay I have tried to do several things. First, I have tried to show that the language of our culture, the ways in which we talk and think about fairness and caring, is sufficient for our being able to treat others fairly or with care much more frequently than we do. The conceptual framework may not yet be sufficiently sophisticated or adequately clear for the resolution of some moral problems, but it does provide enough information for us to act better than we do.

The important part of our understanding of caring that we too frequently ignore is that our attitudes or motives are as important a part of caring as is anything else. Caring for others, as opposed to merely doing something that will in some way help them, requires that we act with the appropriate motive or attitude. Doing something "for" another with the wrong attitude can create fear or pain in the other. What we do "for" the other is canceled out by what we do "to" them by treating them with the wrong attitude.

The important part of our understanding of fairness that we too frequently ignore is that there is no single understanding of fairness or justice that works in all cases. We have different understandings (procedural vs. substantive; liberal vs. free market) of what people deserve and why. These different understandings are appropriate to some circumstances and not others. Deciding which sense of fairness applies to which set of circumstances is a matter of judgment, rather than the application of some single view.

Given the character of caring and of fairness noted above, the opportunity for self-deception to affect our decisions and behavior is considerable. And if we do not properly understand our underlying motivation, we are more likely to treat others unfairly or without care, even though our stated reasoning (rationalization) may include the language of caring or fairness. If we made a mistake in every situation in which we were unsure as to what the right action would be, we would do less harm, I believe, than we do when we claim to be fair or caring, but are in fact deceiving ourselves. We do more harm when what is right or wrong is obvious but we are unable to bring ourselves to act rightly.

In giving examples of cases where I think a lack of self-knowledge has played an important role in the outcome of one's deliberations, I have provided not only examples of teachers' interactions with students, but also examples of teachers interacting with coworkers. I believe that much of our uncaring and unfair behavior in education occurs outside of teacher-student relationships.

Finally, we might argue for a long time about whether I am correct in assessing the examples that I have given. The point of the examples, however, is not to show that I am correct and someone else incorrect in these particular cases, but rather to suggest some areas in which the reader might readily find his or her own examples of self-deception. The areas of status and power seem to me to be likely places to find a lack of self-knowledge affecting our behavior. The areas of sexuality and religion may not be places where the reader will discover self-deception, but they suggest that each of us may have his or her own special areas of self-deception.

The task before each of us, if we want to be more caring in our behavior, if we want to treat others fairly, is to follow the Socratic dictum "Know thyself." This is, I believe, a daunting task and one that must be carried out daily. Any lapse in our self-knowledge can lead to a lack of caring or to the unfair treatment of others. The task of knowing ourselves, however, is the essential ingredient in our behaving well.

REFERENCES

Astin, Alexander W. (1997). Our obsession with being "smart" is distorting intellectual life. *The Chronicle of Higher Education, 44*(5), A60.

Dworkin, Ronald. (1977). *Taking rights seriously.* Cambridge, MA: Harvard University Press.

Gardner, Howard. (1993). *Multiple intelligences.* New York: Basic Books.

Gilligan, Carol. (1982). *In a different voice.* Cambridge, MA: Harvard University Press.

McKeon, Richard. (1941). *The basic works of Aristotle.* New York: Random House.

Noddings, Nel. (1984). *Caring: A feminist approach to ethics and moral education.* Berkeley: University of California Press.

Nozick, Robert. (1974). *Anarchy, state, and utopia.* New York: Basic Books.

Rawls, John. (1971). *A theory of justice.* Cambridge, MA: Harvard University Press.

PART III

Public Policy Issues

CHAPTER 7

School Vouchers in Caring Liberal Communities

Rita C. Manning

Defenders of school vouchers cite their benefit to children and their parents. Critics also focus on the effects on individual children and their parents, noting how money spent on vouchers leaves less for school districts to spend on the remaining students. As a defender of an ethic of care, I agree that schoolchildren and their parents should be a locus of concern, but I am not convinced that keeping them in the center of our thinking means that we must be in favor of school vouchers. I also think there is a neglected strand in the conversation about school vouchers and that is the effect on the larger society. In this chapter, I shall examine the effects on both schoolchildren and the larger society. I shall be using three theoretical lenses: liberalism, communitarianism, and an ethic of care.

An ethic of care is an ethical theory—a way of thinking about what one morally ought to do. Liberalism and communitarianism are political philosophies. One of the central functions of a political philosophy is to help us to think about what a just society would be. There is an obvious connection between ethical theories and political philosophies. An ethical theory tells us what kind of behavior ought to be prohibited in an ideal society and what sort of behavior ought to be encouraged. I use these three theoretical lenses because liberalism (in its classic form) is the founding and still prevailing political philosophy in the United States. It is also the political philosophy that is most clearly compatible with rights and justice based ethics. An ethic of care is an alternative to rights and justice-based ethics and is eminently defensible in its own right. Communitarianism is the political philosophy which is the main alternative to liberalism.

Political philosophies are what Jean-François Lyotard (1984) would call "grand narratives," designed to provide a justification for every political institution and every decision made about social arrangements. But the grandness of the narratives makes it possible to use these frameworks to defend seemingly contradictory outcomes. The strategy of appealing to a political philosophy involves citing its fundamental precepts and then showing how these precepts support or count against a particular social arrangement. As such a grand narrative, liberalism can be used both to defend and critique school vouchers. We shall see that a similar claim can be made about communitarianism.

At this point, one might ask why we should make these grand appeals if they are not decisive. The answer, I think, is that though the appeal can be made by either side in a controversy, stronger arguments can be made on one side or the other. I shall argue that both liberalism and communitarianism can provide compelling arguments against vouchers.

LIBERALISM

Liberalism is the most prevalent political philosophy in the United States. It is also the philosophy upon which our country and its institutions, including our public school system, are founded. The word *liberal* has a set of connotations now that make its use rather confusing. It has come to be understood by many to refer to someone who would advocate a strong government presence in helping people to achieve a minimally decent life. In this discussion, I return to the more basic idea of what a liberal is, an idea that had its genesis in the work of such philosophers as Immanuel Kant, John Locke, and John Stuart Mill. In this sense, a liberal is someone who is concerned with individual rights. Liberals differ on what those rights are, how to prioritize them, and how to adjudicate conflicts between them, but liberty and equality have emerged as the most talked about rights within this liberal tradition.

Though liberals generally share a commitment to equality, they offer differing views of what equality is, why it ought to be part of the just state, and ways in which we might meet this ideal. Liberals also have different ways of reconciling the tension between liberty rights and rights to equality. Libertarians, such as Robert Nozick (1974), for example, argue that if we take liberty rights seriously, we would never interfere in social arrangements, no matter how unequal, which result from legitimate exercises of liberty rights. Others have argued that we must be concerned about equality in a just society and hence must find a way to balance liberty and equality. Bruce Ackerman (1980) provides an account of the liberal state that balances liberty and equality. He argues that both negative rights—rights understood as restrictions on the behavior of others—and positive rights—rights that imply duties to create more equal opportunities—ought to be part of the just liberal state.

Liberalism has usually accepted a distinction between the public arenas and private ones because of its concern to protect the individual exercise of choice. But some feminists—Susan Okin (1990), for example—note that this distinction puts the family, which has been for many women the locus of their experience of injustice, outside the sphere of political debate. Her strategy is to show how liberalism can accommodate these concerns and place the family within the sphere of justice.

Contemporary liberalism, especially since John Rawls's important book *A Theory of Justice* (1971), has generally focused on issues of distributive justice—the rightness or wrongness of competing schemes for distributing benefits and burdens in society. Numerous strategies for distributing benefits and burdens have been argued for by liberals. We shall see that this strand of liberalism is invoked in discussions of vouchers.

Liberals have been debating the existence and compulsory nature of schooling since before public schooling existed. Libertarians can object to compulsory schooling on two grounds. The first is that the family is compelled to send the child to school and the child is compelled to go, regardless of the child's or the family's desires. The second is that if education is to be both compulsory and supported or even provided by the state, then the tax dollars of taxpayers are taken from them in violation of their liberty right to do what they want with them. We can respond to libertarian concerns from within this perspective by pointing out that an educated citizenry is just as important as the police force in maintaining order.

But other sorts of liberals have concerns about compulsory schooling, too. John Stuart Mill (1854/1984), for example, did not dispute the compulsory nature of education, but argued that the parents, and not the state, should decide the content of that education. He added that the state should subsidize families who can not afford private schooling, thus making him appear to be a very early advocate of vouchers. Still, it is important to keep in mind Mill's insistence that the state "is bound to maintain a vigilant control over his [any particular citizen's] exercise of any power which it allows him to possess over others" (p. 175). He cites the power of husbands and fathers over wives and children as the paradigm case of this exercise of power. "It is in the case of children that misapplied notions of liberty are a real obstacle to the fulfillment by the state of its duties" (p. 175). He specifies that one of the state's duties with respect to children is to see that each father provide each child "an education fitting him to perform his part well in life toward others and toward himself" (p. 176). No adult will perform well, according to Mill, unless he is free: "The only freedom which deserves the name is that of pursuing our own good in our own way, so long as we do not attempt to deprive others of theirs or impede their efforts to obtain it" (p. 72). It follows that the state has a duty to compel parents who can afford to educate their children to give their children an education that will allow them to make their own choices and act upon them. It has the additional duty of providing a similar education for the children of families that cannot afford to provide it themselves.

David Kirkpatrick (1990), a contemporary defender of vouchers, offers an additional appeal to liberal values when he argues that parents have a right to decide on the education of their children. "Certainly a parent who can decide whether or not a child will have an operation . . . should be able to decide . . . what educational methods he or she prefers . . ." (p. 49).

The appeal is problematic for several reasons. First, it assumes, wrongly, that parents *do* have moral and/or legal rights to decide whether their children will have an operation. Parents who have refused to consent to surgery for a life-threatening condition (preferring to pray instead, for example) have been compelled to submit the child for medical care and this compulsion is morally justified by appeal to the best interests of the child. In many states, minors can get abortions without parental consent. This is usually defended on the basis of a right to privacy. Second, this emphasis on the rights of the parents suggests that it is the parent's rights which are paramount here, and not the child's. Liberals have argued that children have the relevant rights in these cases and that parents have an obligation to act as agents for their children (Cohen, 1980). In the case of education, Cornel Hamm (1982) argues that children have a "right to rational autonomous agency" and that their parents have a "duty to provide an education leading to rational autonomy" (p. 71). Amy Guttman (1980) argues that the content of education "will depend upon what is adequate for living a full life within their society—for being capable of choosing among available conceptions of the good and of participating intelligently in democratic politics" (p. 340). Hamm (1982) argues that this requires a content mandated by the majority because it is only when we put all our heads together that we can figure out what our children really need to know in order to exercise their rational autonomy.

Autonomy is a much discussed notion by liberal political philosophers, but the core notion is that the autonomous individual can make free choices and act on them (Dworkin, 1988). Defenders of vouchers often make appeals to autonomy, pointing out that parents ought to be free to send their children to the school of their choice (Spoerl, 1995). This is a limited appeal, however, for it fails to attend to the autonomy of the children. If children are to become adults capable of making free choices, they must have an education that makes this possible. So if defenders of vouchers want to appeal consistently to liberalism in defense of vouchers, they must insist that vouchers be used to support only schools that focus on a liberal education; that is, an education designed to ensure that its graduates can make free, informed choices and act upon them. Not all private schools fit this bill. Not all public schools live up to this ideal, either, but I would argue that this ideal both is part of the heritage of public schooling in this country and remains a vital force in many of our public schools. When and where our public schools fail to attend to the autonomy of students, committed liberals are obliged to protest.

Defenders of school vouchers have made other appeals to liberalism which focus not on the rights of the parents, but on the good of the students (Harmer, 1994). The argument typically takes the following form. Many of our public schools are not properly educating students. In our highly complex technological society, a good K–12 education is an absolute requirement for entrance and success in higher education, and some education beyond high school is essential if one is to have a reasonably comfortable and meaningful life. School vouchers are an important strategy in the battle to improve schools. Finally, one might make an appeal to a principle of distributive justice. A good education is an important social good, and it is now distributed unequally and without regard to need or merit. Providing school vouchers to families who cannot now afford private school would be a more just distribution of educational benefits.

The liberal counter argument can agree that each student needs and perhaps even has a right to a decent K–12 education (Katz, 1996). However, there is a great deal of controversy about whether our public schools are really failing to give students a decent education (Smith & Meier, 1995). In addition, any liberal defense of vouchers must agree to two central elements of liberalism. The first, as we have seen, is the value of autonomy, and the second is liberalism's vision of the good society.

Liberals disagree about many of the details, but a core notion of the good liberal society is a society which defends the liberty of its autonomous members. So a liberal defender of vouchers must insist that vouchers be used only to support schools designed to achieve two goals: the rational autonomy of the students, and the continued commitment of the students to the value of liberty. Critics of vouchers need not and indeed do not argue that our public schools are all wonderful, and here is a place where liberalism provides guidance for improving public schools—they should have autonomy as a guiding principle, and they should aim at educating students who will be active members of a flourishing liberal society. Unless defenders of vouchers are willing to embrace this ideal, they cannot consistently appeal to liberal values in defense of vouchers.

There are additional liberal criticisms which can, and indeed have, been made, to this "liberal" defense of vouchers. One criticism is that providing vouchers will most likely result in less money being available to public schools, and public schools are already operating on a shoestring. This will result in a great disparity of education available to those who choose vouchers and those who remain in public schools because they still cannot afford private school, or because of parental inability to navigate the system or the child's disabilities and so forth. Other principles of distributive justice can be brought to bear which buttress this concern that the distribution of education which would result from most vouchers schemes is unequal. These arguments rest on an empirical claim which, if true, provides a liberal with serious grounds for concern about vouchers.

Communitarianism is perhaps a horse of a different color. Though communitarians come in a wide variety, the central tenet is that we should value communities. This is a fairly innocuous condition, however, and fails to distinguish communitarianism from any other plausible political philosophy, any of which ought to recognize the value of human communities. For the purposes of this paper, I shall sketch and defend several versions of communitarianism, two of which are compatible with an ethic of care. First, though, I shall need to say a bit about an ethic of care.

CARING AS AN ETHICAL PERSPECTIVE

An ethic of care is both a way of being in the world and a more or less systematic exploration and justification of moral decisions. As a way of being in the world, an ethic of care as I understand it is characterized by the following features: moral attention, sympathetic understanding, relationship awareness, and response. I shall discuss each of these in turn. In order to present each feature with optimal clarity, I shall assume a situation in which there are two persons. Let us then suppose that I am in my office when a student who is struggling in my class comes for extra help and that I am committed and able to respond in a caring way.

Moral attention is the attention to the situation in all its complexity. When I am morally attentive, I wish to become aware of all the details that will allow me to respond to the situation with sympathetic understanding. In this case, I attend carefully to my student. I try to ascertain how he is doing in the class and why. I do not assume that he is stupid, lazy, or otherwise at fault (though I may *later* come to believe that he is at fault), but listen as he explains what he does not understand and try to guide him both to a solution and to a new sense of confidence about the material.

When I sympathetically understand the situation, I am open to sympathizing and even identifying with the persons in the situation. I try to be aware of what the others in the situation would want me to do, what would most likely be in their best interests, and how they would like me to carry out their wishes and interests. I call this attention to the best interests of others "maternalism." It is done in the context of a special sensitivity to the wishes of the other and with an understanding of the other's interest that is shaped by a deep sympathy and understanding. To return to my student—I begin by pushing aside my annoyance at being interrupted and try to see him sympathetically. If I feel it hard to be sympathetic, I may try several strategies—perhaps imagining him as myself in an earlier academic struggle. As I adopt this sympathetic attitude, I become aware of what he wants and needs from me. Finally, I look to satisfy his need in a way that will preserve his sense of competence.

There is a special kind of relationship awareness that characterizes an ethic of care. I recognize that the other is in relationship with me. First, there is the most basic relationship, that of fellow creatures. Second, there is the immediate relationship of need and ability to fill the need. Finally, I may be in some role relationship with the other that calls for a particular response, such as teacher-student. I am aware of all these relationships as I survey a situation from the perspective of an ethic of care. But there is another kind of relationship awareness that is involved as well. I am aware of the network of relationships that connect humans, and I care about preserving and nurturing these relationships. So I see my student as a fellow human and a fellow learner. I recognize that he is in need of my help and that I am able to give it. I recognize my role as teacher and the special obligation this implies. Next, I see him as a member of the classroom community and the university. Finally, I acknowledge the web of personal relationships that can either support or undermine his academic success. As I search for ways to help him, I do so with the desire to strengthen all these relationships.

Finally, an ethic of care requires a response on my part. It is not enough to stare at my student and imagine him in a sympathetic way, to see our relationship as well as the myriad of relationships that connect him to others. I must make my caring concrete in the actions that I take to respond to his need.

Care and Vouchers

We can now draw some conclusions about an ethic of care and vouchers. First, we should keep our moral attention on students and their parents. We should try to understand sympathetically all students and parents. Caring for students requires a special kind of attention from teachers and administrators, as Nel Noddings (1984) describes in rich detail. But caring for students requires more than a style of interaction. It also requires giving children a real opportunity to develop the abilities and motivation to learn, both for their own growth and so that they will be able to have jobs which will allow them to care for themselves and their families. Obviously many schools, both public and private, do not treat students in caring ways. A caring response requires moving schools toward more caring models, in a way that nurtures and sustains the communities that constitute our schools and the communities in which they are embedded.

One might argue that vouchers will be just the strategy for bringing this about. Perhaps. But a defender of an ethic of care would need to be convinced that vouchers would provide this for all our children. The concerns about the effects of vouchers which were cited in the discussion of liberalism can be brought to bear here as well. In addition, communities play a significant role in an ethic of care, so we need to see the effect of vouchers on our various interrelated communities.

Care and Communitarianism

There are two basic reasons why defenders of an ethic of care put special value on communities. One is that connected selves, those who most naturally understand the moral universe in terms of an ethic of care, value the relationships which are available in healthy communities because they want to protect the ties of affection which they value greatly and which are a source of their self-identity. Second, an ethic of care understands all persons as embedded in a network of relationships. Thus no successful response to need is possible without creating, maintaining and invoking the kind of stable, concerned relationships which can exist only in healthy communities.

But this concern with community is compatible with a sophisticated liberalism. A liberal may argue for a strong community in order better to provide individuals with the social goods they desire. If we add that persons are, at least in part, constituted by their relations with others, then this kind of liberalism is compatible with an ethic of care. The crucial difference between this kind of liberalism and communitarianism lies in the value of the community and the individual's obligation to his or her community.

Some defenders of an ethic of care argue that we have obligations only to those to whom we are already in some kind of relation. I would argue that an ethic of care requires us to value all humans (Manning, 1992). Communities play different roles in these two different versions of an ethic of care.

Defenders of what I shall call here a "limited ethic of care" could value communities for the additional reason that they already include all the important relationships in a community member's life. Defenders of what I shall call a "universal ethic of care" will also value communities but do not think that our moral obligations are exhausted merely by our taking care of our duties to our fellow community members.

COMMUNITARIANISM AND VOUCHERS

Some communitarians, notably Alasdair MacIntyre (1984), argue that patriotism is the most important virtue a person can have. Though MacIntyre had much smaller political entities in mind, (e.g., Greek city-states), some current defenders of patriotism would insist on loyalty to the nation. I shall call this version of communitarianism "nationalistic communitarianism." There are two features of this version of communitarianism. The first is that loyalty to one's community is more important than loyalty to any particular person. The second is that the nation is the proper object of our patriotic zeal.

Nationalistic communitarianism would seem to be incompatible with vouchers. Though MacIntyre seems to prefer earlier societies (he cites the ancient Greeks with some approval), he does argue that any flourishing society must make its values the values of all its citizens. The United States is a liberal democratic society, and the values which underlie our institutions are transmitted, in part, through our system of public education. If we are to maintain our status as a liberal democracy, we can adopt only educational schemes that transmit liberal values. This does not rule out all voucher schemes, but it does provide a litmus test—those schools teaching values that are in conflict with the liberal values of the United States will not be supported by vouchers. Now it is precisely an uneasiness with just these values that motivates some private-school adherents to argue for vouchers. On MacIntyre's grounds, they will not be in the running for state funds.

In addition, this version of communitarianism is not compatible with either a limited ethic of care or a universal one, since it places loyalty to an abstract entity, the state, over loyalty to family and friends. Neither does it appear to be compatible with rights-and-justice–based ethics, with their focus on the moral priority of the individual.

But communitarians need not defend the nation state as the only viable community. Rousseau (1762/1994), for example, shares MacIntyre's assessment of the value of loyalty, but along with MacIntyre, he envisions much smaller nations. And nations, regardless of size, are legitimate "bodies politic," in Rousseau's words, only when they further the goal which motivated humans to form societies in the first place—the protection of each of its citizens. This version of communitarianism also includes shared values and a commitment by each member to the survival of the community. Though Rousseau imagined small nations as the premier body politic, other communitarians can and do offer other close-knit communities as the paradigm communities. This version of communitarianism, which I shall call "*close-knit communitarianism*," is compatible with a limited ethic of care.

I suspect that many defenders of vouchers, whether they would describe themselves this way or not, are communitarians of similar ilk. They wish to send their children to private school so they can influence their children to be members of communities which are not identical to the community of citizens of the United States. (These communities may be based on social and economic class, religion, national origin, and so on.) They can appeal to communitarianism to defend vouchers. Communities exist in large part because of their values, and if communities are to continue to exist, they must be able to transmit these values to future members. This can be done only in the context of institutions which share the values of the communities. They can also appeal to a limited ethic of care. My community is composed of all my family and friends and all those I am likely to have in the future. In caring for my community, I am making sure that networks will exist to care for my family and friends.

These are perhaps compelling arguments and ought to persuade members of these communities of their obligations to each other, but it is not clear to me why another community, namely, the citizens of the United States or the citizens of a particular state, has any obligation to support these other communities. Second, benefiting these other communities may well be costly to those who are not members of these communities. If we think that an ethic of care requires that we be open to sympathetic understanding to all humans, then we will want to take a long, hard look at the effects of any distribution of resources.

Finally, it does seem to me that when we make any decision about vouchers, we should seriously consider the perspective of the community of citizens and potential citizens of the United States, since it is a decision that will profoundly affect the future of this country.

Some communitarian defenders of vouchers are sensitive to these concerns. Clifford Cobb (1992) argues that close-knit communities are required for the stability of the larger political community. He offers several arguments: that it is only in the interchange of diverse perspectives in a small close-knit community that we come to respect tolerance in the larger soci-

ety; that a commitment solely to a national community makes for a belli-
cose community; that we learn the altruism that is required in national communities through the self-sacrifice we must practice in our own communities. Iris Young (1990) offers a similar vision of communitarianism, though
not in the context of school vouchers. She defends an "ideal of politics as
deliberation in a heterogeneous public which affirms group differences and
gives specific representation to oppressed groups" (p. 260).

This version of communitarianism, which I call "connected-communities communitarianism," is more promising than the other versions of
communitarianism. It respects our intuitions that there is value both in
our close-knit communities and in our larger political communities. It is
also compatible with an ethic of care which focuses on our obligation to
be caring toward all humans, though we may carry out this obligation in
different ways, depending upon group membership.

However, it is not obvious that connected-communities communitarianism is compatible with a voucher system. First, this view cannot embrace any social arrangement that will undercut its focus on close-knit community and political community in harmony and interrelatedness. I share
Rousseau's concern about the stability of political communities dominated
by close-knit groups. I also share Young's belief that we define ourselves
largely by our participation in close-knit communities. Retaining both our
self-identities and stable political communities requires careful thought and
commitment on our part, in addition to specific "psychological disposi-
tion(s), cultural expressions, and political institutions" (Young, 1990, p. 260).

It is not obvious that public schooling is sensitive to the need to vali-
date group difference at the same time as it provides a foundation for
political stability, but there is some reason for optimism. The focus on
multiculturalism that is emerging in some of our public schools, coupled
with the state and federal influence and the influence of the electorate on
schools, gives me some reason to hope that public schools at least understand this as part of their mission. I feel no such assurance about private
schools, which have different missions and histories. Connected communities communitarianism could not embrace vouchers unless the private
schools benefiting from such a program could demonstrate that they are
making serious attempts to achieve this dual goal.

CARE, COMMUNITARIANISM, AND VOUCHERS

I have argued that there are two versions of communitarianism which
are compatible with an ethic of care: close-knit communitarianism, and
connected-communities communitarianism. Close-knit communitarian-

ism can be cited as a rationale for vouchers. Close-knit communitarianism, however, is most naturally defended by appeal to a limited ethic of care— an ethic that understands moral obligation exclusively in terms of obligations to members of one's close-knit community. I find a limited ethic of care problematic precisely because it does limit my obligations in this way; I want an ethic to be compatible with my strong intuition that I do have some obligations to strangers. Hence I think that a universal ethic of care is a more defensible version of an ethic of care. Connected-communities communitarianism appears to be compatible with universal care. However, this view can offer only a limited defense of vouchers. A voucher system, on this view, must support the psychological dispositions, cultural expressions, and political institutions of a liberal democracy committed to valuing, respecting, and negotiating difference as members of a shared political community. In addition, a universal ethic of care requires that all children be given a caring education. It is an empirical question whether vouchers actually do this, but the concern that some children (namely, those who are left behind in underfunded public schools) are not granted such an education would loom as a very large impediment to an endorsement by a universal ethic of care.

CONCLUSION

I have argued that there are serious concerns, drawn from liberal political philosophy, communitarianism, and a universal ethic of care, about school vouchers. Liberalism questions the ability of such a system of education to deliver equal access to education, a foundation for adult autonomy, and the transmission of liberal values to future generations. A universal ethic of care focuses on the effect of such a system on all children, those who would use vouchers and those who would be left in public schools. Connected-communities communitarianism would be concerned about whether vouchers could achieve the goal of validating group difference while providing a foundation for political stability.

None of what I have said so far is to be taken as a blanket defense of our public school system. There is no question that the public school system is failing large numbers of children in just the ways that trouble liberalism, communitarianism, and an ethic of care. Liberalism, communitarianism, and an ethic of care each have a critique of this failure and prescriptions for changing it to success. There is clearly much work to be done. What is not so clear is whether vouchers should be part of the solution.

At best, liberalism could endorse a voucher system limited to schools that transmitted liberal values and nurtured the autonomy of students, as long as the existence of such a system did not undermine the education of students who did not participate in the voucher system. Connected-communities communitarianism would insist on support of close-knit communities in the context of a stable political community. An ethic of care would add that each student deserves to be treated with care and to be given an education which would allow him or her to live a life of dignity and care. An ethic of care would also share liberal and communitarian concerns about the larger community, though for different reasons. Liberalism is committed to the continued existence of a liberal society. Communitarianism is committed to the flourishing of close-knit communities within a stable political community. An ethic of care is committed to the existence of a flourishing community in which the demands of care are met. Could a voucher system be drafted which would address these concerns? Perhaps, but I believe I have shown that the burden of proof is on defenders of school vouchers.

REFERENCES

Ackerman, Bruce. (1980). *Social justice in the liberal state*. New Haven, CT: Yale University Press.

Cobb, Clifford. (1992). *Responsive schools, renewed communities*. San Francisco: ICS Press.

Cohen, Howard. (1980). *Equal rights for children*. Totowa, NJ: Littlefield, Adams.

Gilligan, Carol. (1982). *In a different voice*. Cambridge, MA: Harvard University Press.

Dworkin, Gerald. (1988). *The theory and practice of autonomy*. New York: Cambridge University Press.

Guttman, Amy. (1980). Children, paternalism, and education: a liberal argument. *Philosophy and Public Affairs*, *9*(4), 338–358

Hamm, Cornell. (1982). Constraints on parents' rights. In Michael Manley-Cassimir (Ed.), *Family choice in schooling* (pp. 71–84). Lexington, MA: Lexington Books.

Harmer, David. (1994). *School choice*. Washington, DC: Cato Institute.

Katz, Michael. (1996). Equal educational opportunity: reexamining a liberal ideal. In Rita Manning & Rene Trujillo (Eds.), *Social justice in a diverse society* (pp. 39–46). Mountain View, CA: Mayfield Press.

Kirkpatrick, David. (1990). *Choice in schooling*. Chicago: Loyola University Press.

Kohlberg, Lawrence. (1981). *The philosophy of moral development*. New York: Harper & Row.

Lyotard, Jean-François. (1984). *The postmodern condition: A report on knowledge* (Geoff Bennington & Brian Massumi, trans.). Minneapolis: University of Minnesota Press.

Lyons, Nona. (1983). Two perspectives on self, relationship, and morality. *Harvard Educational Review*, *53*, 125–145.

MacIntyre, Alasdair. (1984). Is patriotism a virtue? Lawrence: University of Kansas, Philosophy Department.

Manning, Rita. (1992). *Speaking from the heart: A feminist perspective on ethics.* Lanham MD: Rowman and Littlefield.

Mill, John Stuart. (1984). *On liberty.* New York: Penguin Books. (Original work published 1854.)

Noddings, Nel. (1984). *Caring: A feminine approach to ethics and moral education.* Berkeley: University of California Press.

Nozick, Robert. (1974). *Anarchy, state, and utopia.* New York: Basic Books.

Okin, Susan Moller. (1990). *Justice, gender, and family.* New York: Harper Collins.

Rawls, John. (1971). *A theory of justice.* Cambridge, MA: Harvard University Press.

Rousseau, Jean-Jacques. (1994). *The social contract* (Christopher Betts, Trans.). Oxford: Oxford University Press. (Original work published 1762)

Smith, Kevin, & Meier, Kenneth. (1995). *The case against school choice.* Armonk, NY: M. E. Sharpe.

Spoerl, Joseph. (1995). Justice and the case for school vouchers. *Public Affairs Quarterly, 9,* 75–86.

Young, Iris Marion. (1990). *Justice and the politics of difference.* Princeton, NJ: Princeton University Press.

CHAPTER 8

Ethnicity, Identity, and Community

Lawrence Blum

Disputes about the the appropriate roles of care and justice in ethics and moral development theory have made little contact with another area of contemporary controversy, multiculturalism in schools and society. Yet the two have much to offer one another. Ethnic cultures and ethnic identities can provide a form of moral orientation for their members. But this moral orientation takes the form of a group consciousness that does not fall comfortably into either side of the care/justice debate. It is neither as individual in its focus as care nor as universalist as justice. Thus the group aspect of ethno-cultural identity challenges the idea that care and justice together exhaust the entire moral terrain (Blum, 1994). At the same time, norms of care and justice do appropriately govern aspects of ethnicity-based moral consciousness and community.

Multiculturalism is frequently criticized as divisive. The emphasis on ethnic or racial identity—for example, ethnic affirmation in multicultural curricula, in-group ethnic socializing, and institutional support of ethno-racially based dormitories and organizations—is claimed to be harmful to unity and community. *Difference* is privileged at the expense of *commonality*.

Yet *proponents* of multiculturalism, too, invoke community in their defense of ethno-racial social and cultural affirmation in colleges. Members of ethno-racial groups (a term I define below) seek realization of a sense of community with their fellow ethnics and desire recognition for that ethnicity-based community from the wider institutions and bodies of which those groups are a constituent part.

The stances of both opponents and proponents of multiculturalism make this dispute quite difficult to resolve. Each tends, at least implicitly, to make two problematic assumptions. The first is that intra- and inter-ethnic communities are necessarily in tension with one another; loyalty to one necessarily diminishes or compromises loyalty to or involvement in the other.

The second assumption is that there is something suspect about one or another of the types of community in question. Multiculturalists, though often paying some kind of homage (or, less charitably, lip service) to the importance of trans-ethnic communities—both large (national) and small (schools, classes, neighborhoods)—generally accord primacy to ethno-racial communities and identities. Multiculturalist writing is often suspicious of communities with aspirations to trans-ethnicity or universality for employing a false universality to mask cultural bias toward or against particular ethno-racial groups in the mix in question (Scott, 1995). Critics of multiculturalism who are concerned about community tend to do precisely the reverse. They may reluctantly concede some value to intra-ethnic community, but they give strong pride of place to non-ethnic and trans-ethnic communities. (Some critics of multiculturalism are not concerned about trans-ethnic community, but about individuality or a perceived anti-Western or anti-American bias.)

Both of these assumptions are unfounded. Healthy forms of identification with one's ethnic community are entirely consistent with identification with trans-ethnic communities; group attachments do not fit the zero-sum model. Moreover, both types of community do, or can, embody important values.

In this chapter I will be concerned mostly with the second issue—specifically, with values realized by intra-ethnic communities. I will argue that intra-ethnic communities come in several distinct forms, and realize distinct values, some of which are distinct from both care and justice.

Debates about multiculturalism are often framed in an abstract and over-polarized manner—difference versus commonality, giving voice to marginalized voices versus imposition of dominant culture, individualism versus communitarianism, and the like. This chapter is an attempt to shed light on one small part of this complex terrain, in hope of thereby encouraging a more nuanced and substantive discussion of the many other issues involved as well.

ETHNO-RACIAL IDENTITIES: A TYPOLOGY

I will adopt David Hollinger's (1995) term *ethno-racial* to refer to major groupings currently conceptualized when people discuss ethnic groups in schools and colleges in the United States—African Americans, Native Americans, Latinos/Hispanics, European Americans, Asian Americans. The term *ethno-racial* captures the complex character of these groups, in which racial and ethno-cultural elements interweave in forming the group identity. It is meant to suggest, too, that those two factors each have shifting meanings, ones that preclude a sharp distinction between them.

The five ethno-racial groups listed above are by no means the only ones currently visible in educational institutions. One finds subgroups of each—a campus with a Korean-American organization, or Haitian-American club, for example—or, in the other direction, formations and organizations of "people of color," encompassing the above ethno-racial groups other than European Americans. Much of the subsequent discussion will apply to both these sub- and supra-ethno-racial groups. Nevertheless, what Hollinger calls the "ethno-racial pentagon" constitutes the dominant divisions and group categorizations in most high schools and colleges, and in recent popular consciousness.

Students bring differing types of ethno-racial cultures from their home backgrounds to these educational institutions. I will distinguish *four* forms of ethno-racial identity. The list is not exhaustive; but it suggests a range of forms materially relevant to the character of ethno-racial communities in educational institutions—to the values they are able to realize, to their impact on possibilities for trans-ethnic community in an institution, and for how issues of care and justice are pertinent to these communities.

Thick Ethnicity

"Thick" ethnicity contrasts with thin ethnicity, though the distinction is only a matter of degree. Thick/thin concerns the extent to which one's daily life is immersed in and permeated by one's ethno-racial identity. Criteria of thick ethnicity in a student's home background include the following: living in a mono-ethnic neighborhood; coming from a family which speaks a language other than English; attending largely mono-ethnic schools; having a family life permeated with ethnicity-based rituals and other cultural expressions of ethnicity (music, food, and the like); being able to speak the (non-English) language of one's parents or grandparents; being immersed in the ethnicity-based (including religious) traditions of one's ethnic group; having friends almost solely from one's ethnic group.

Thin Ethnicity

"Thin" ethnicity is marked by what sociologists often call "symbolic ethnicity" (Gans, 1996). Mary Waters (1990) studied this form of ethnicity among second- and third-generation White Catholic ethnics in her book

Ethnic Options. She prefers the term *voluntary ethnicity* as allowing for a genuine personal meaningfulness called into question by Gans's analysis.

Thinly ethnic persons partake of some cultural and familial aspects of their ethno-cultures, but do not live or go to school primarily among members of their ethno-racial groups. Their ethnicity is not very salient in their daily existence. The distinction between thin and thick carries with it no implication that thick ethnicity is more "authentic" or "real" than thin ethnicity, though thick ethnics (and others) often regard thin ethnicity in that way.

Factors empirically affecting the thinness or thickness of one's ethnicity are immigrant status, distance in time from ancestors' immigration, and economic position; if all other things are equal, thick ethnicity is found in poorer and immigrant families, thin ethnicity in families more well-to-do and more distant from original immigration. However, these relations hold only in general. There are many exceptions. African Americans as a group provide several exceptions to these links. Because residential segregation is greater among middle-class African Americans than among any other prominent ethno-racial group's middle class (Hacker, 1995, ch. 3), African-American young people are likely to be more thickly ethnic across class lines than are other groups. Moreover, though African Americans are native English speakers, the linguistic form sometimes called "black English" provides a linguistic counterpart to non-English languages among other thickly ethnic groups. Speaking only black English or standard English that is heavily inflected with black English is a marker (though only one among several others) of thick ethnicity among African Americans. Speaking *only* standard English is one marker of thin ethnicity. Moving easily between the two, depending on context, might place one somewhere in the middle, other factors aside.

Identity Ethnicity

Identity ethnicity is an ethno-racial identification with no cultural content. Though perhaps an extreme case, it is significantly conceptually distinct from both thin and thick ethnicity. African-American, Latino-American, Asian-American, and Native-American are all very salient social identities in the United States, and identification of someone as a member of such groups can be marked by features other than culture—for example, by phenotypic features taken as corresponding to a "racial" manner of understanding such groups, or by ancestry as a member of the group. For these reasons, someone may be identified as, and may identify herself as, a member of one of these groups, even if she has partaken of virtually no aspect of the ethno-culture seen as corresponding to that group (see also Appiah, 1996; Hollinger, 1995).

Imagine, for example, a third generation Japanese American growing up in an (otherwise) all-white suburb. Her family is completely assimilated, at least to the extent of not observing any distinct Japanese rituals, not preparing Japanese foods, and not expressing any distinct identification or interest in Japan or with other Japanese Americans. The girl has never explored Japanese culture; her own peer culture is the multicultural mix we call "American culture," and her family culture is barely distinguishable from that of her white neighbors. Nevertheless, because the girl "looks Asian" (within the U.S. context) and because her ancestors are unquestionably Japanese-American, she can, and in fact is likely to, be taken as Asian-American or Japanese-American.

When this young woman comes to college, she meets substantial numbers of Asian-American students for the first time. Despite the absence of any distinct ethno-culture, she is able to identify herself as an "Asian American." That identity can be or become meaningful to her, and will often be accepted by others as "legitimate." She may (come to) feel a real bond with other Asian Americans, including those who are much more culturally ethnic (thick or thin) than she.

Mary Waters's (1990) account of ethnicity strongly emphasizes an asymmetry between white and non-white ethnicity in regard to the degree of choice one has to distance oneself from one's ethnic (or, in my terminology, ethno-racial) group identity or not. A Polish American can generally choose when to exhibit, celebrate, or take on, her ethnicity. She is not visibly a Polish American and may not have a characteristically Polish name. African Americans and Asian Americans (with the exception of the few able to "pass" as white) do not have this option. They are treated *as* African-American, or Asian-American, as illustrated in the above example.

This point is relevant to the possibilities for identity ethnicity. What allows for identity ethnicity is the social salience and significance of the identity category. Physical appearance, shared history as groups seen and treated as distinctive, and the self-claiming (intensified in the past three decades) of their ethno-racial identity as a group have all contributed to the salience of non-white ethno-racial group identity in the United States, thus providing the conceptual and psychological space for an individual to take on an ethnic *social* identity without having the *cultural* substance often assumed to accompany it.

It is useful to distinguish among three distinct types of identity ethnic:

1. A person who recognizes that she is seen by others, and would be classified by the governing classificatory conventions in the society, as a member of ethnicity E, but who does not herself identify personally as an E.

2. A "pure" identity ethnic, who makes the distinction I am drawing here, and so regards herself as *not* having an ethno-culture (though perhaps aspires to have one, or wishes she had one), yet, unlike type (1), does personally identify with (identify herself as) ethnicity E.
3. Identity ethnics who do not themselves subjectively make a clear distinction between an identity ethnic (one without cultural ethnicity) and a cultural (thin or thick) ethnic. Persons in this category think of the ethno-culture of their ethnic identity as something that belongs to them, but which they perhaps need to "discover," or get in touch with.

Anti-discrimination Ethnicity

The fourth type of ethno-racial identity is grounded entirely in the ethnic group's being a target of discrimination. In the ideal type I am imagining, the individual is not and does not regard herself as *culturally* ethnic at all. But she feels a strong loyalty to and identification with her group because and insofar as it suffers discrimination at the hands of others. That identification is experienced and manifested most strongly *when the group is discriminated against*; but it also exists as a standing identification.

The anti-discrimination ethnic is thus one subgroup within identity ethnics of type 2 (a person who identifies with her ethnic group, but does not regard the identification as something grounded in a shared culture). For the anti-discrimination ethnic it is the ethnic group not as a *cultural* group but as a *discriminated-against* group that is the source of her identification.

For the most part, *pure* anti-discrimination ethnic identity is found only in non-white groups (in the United States), for they are by far the most frequent targets of racial and ethnic discrimination. For example, a Mexican American who feels so far removed from Mexican or Mexican-American culture that she has no identification with it might still identify herself clearly *as* Mexican-American and *with* other Mexican Americans insofar as they suffer discrimination.

However, Jews are a "white" group (see also Kaye-Kantrowitz, 1996) that also suffers discrimination, and many Jews' form of identification with Jewish ethnicity is through an anti-discrimination consciousness. Moreover, in specific locales, some other white ethnic groups may be widespread targets of discrimination by other white and non-white ethnic groups. Also, because anti-discrimination ethnicity is subjectively defined, an individual person can adopt it when actual discrimination is non-existent or trivial—thus the possibility of a Euro-American (or white, depending on whether a [quasi-]cultural or a racial dimension is being emphasized) anti-discrimination ethnicity.

The anti-discrimination ethnic is motivated by a justice-based consciousness. But the justice is not of the pure Kohlbergian kind; it is not simply a universal principle to which the ethnic adheres. There are two differences. First, the anti-discriminator's sense of justice is particularized to her own group. While she may well have a broader sense of justice, that is a different matter. She is indignant when her own group, or one of its members, is unjustly treated but does not necessarily have a similar reaction when members of other groups are similarly mistreated.

Second, the anti-discriminator possesses a sense of particularistic connection and bond with members of her group. To her they are not simply *fellow human beings* unjustly treated, but members of her particular ethnoracial group. She feels a distinct, and particular, bond with them.

These two features do not, however, make the anti-discrimination ethnic any less motivated, in her solidarity, by a sense of *justice*. It simply means that this justice is not of a pure Kohlbergian or Kantian type. (This does not mean, however, that it is a species of "care," either, as we will see below.)

Identities and Identifications

A form of anti-discrimination identification can exist not as a pure type of identity ethnicity but as a component of identification that can coexist with cultural identification of either thin or thick variety. In fact, most people of color do possess some combination of cultural and anti-discrimination identifications.

The categories of "thin" and "thick" (ethnic) differ from those of "identity" and "anti-discrimination" in one significant respect. The latter are *chosen*, or at least *affirmed*, ethnic identifications; in fact, in common parlance they would not be seen as forms of ethnicity (or ethnic identity) at all, since that concept implies some cultural content. They are rather forms of ethnic identification. While *membership* in the ethnoracial group in question is not chosen but is (or is at least regarded as) a given—one just *is* Jewish, or African-American, or Mexican-American—nevertheless, whether one *identifies oneself with* that group (in anti-discrimination or other identity modes) is something one chooses, or embraces.

By contrast, thinness and thickness do not express ways an individual has chosen to identify herself. Rather, they express cultural material with which she has been provided. A person brought up in a thick ethnic environment may well recognize herself *as* an E (substitute your favorite thick ethnicity), but she may wish she were not. She may even hate being an E, see it as very confining, and wish to escape it. In any case, she does not embrace E-ness. If she were to be introduced to the distinction between thin ethnicity and thick ethnicity, she might see herself as a thick ethnic who wishes she were a thin ethnic, or wishes she were not an E at all. Thin ethnicity is less permeating of one's life, so in a sense there is less to reject or resent. Still, a thinly ethnic E may wish she were not E; she may not like whatever it is that she associates with (thin) E-ness. She may also wish she were thickly ethnic, yet feel she never can be.

So anti-discrimination and other forms of identity (ethnicity) refer to modes of appropriating identities, while thin and thick refer to the cultural character of the identities themselves, independent of what attitude or claim the individual takes up toward it.

On a given campus, any ethno-racial group present in more than very small numbers is likely to encompass examplars of all four types of ethnicity. Ethno-racial groupings on campuses can be classified as *visible* or *classificatory*. The visible group comprises those group members who distinctly identify with other members of the group, tend to hang out with them, and, more generally, give it to be understood by the wider institution that they are members of the (Asian-American, Latino, etc.) group on campus.

The classificatory group is broader than the visible group and comprises all individuals who would be officially classified as members of the given ethno-racial group, even if they do not actually identify with the visible ethno-racial community on the campus. So this larger group also comprises individuals who do not identify with the specific other Es on the campus, even if each acknowledges herself as an E. The extent to which a classificatory ethnic is also a visible ethnic on a given campus can be a matter of degree and imprecision. Some people will more clearly be members of the visible ethnic group than others.

The classificatory ethno-racial group is likely to include persons of all four types of ethnicity (and some who fit none of those categories). It is possible for the visible community as well to include all four types (though not type 1 of the identity ethnic—the person who disidentifies with her classificatory ethno-racial group). The visible ethno-community is somewhat less likely to include anti-discrimination ethnics, however, as they feel no cultural proclivity with fellow ethnics. Moreover, the visible ethnic community must contain at least some, and often a preponderance, of thin and thick ethnics, since generally a pure identity ethnic comes to think of herself as ethnic only when confronted with other fellow ethnics who possess some cultural substance.

THE "SENSE OF COMMUNITY": A TYPOLOGY

It is sometimes assumed that persons who identify with a given ethnicity necessarily constitute a community with other members of that ethnic group. Depending on what we take "community" to mean, this should not be assumed, as the distinction between "visible" and "classificatory" ethnicity indicates. Suppose, for example, that Jose is a thinly ethnic Mexican American on a campus in which the other Mexican Americans are thickly ethnic. His identity as a Mexican American is not in question, but he may feel no sense of community with the other Mexican Americans (Navarrette, 1993). So (*ethno-racial*) *identity* is not the same as (*ethno-racial*) *community*.

However, where ethnic community *does* exist, what kinds of values do such communities realize? Little systematic thought has been given to this question. Both multiculturalists and anti-multiculturalists trade on the honorific associations of the term *community* (in each of their two favored forms—intra-ethnic and inter-ethnic). But why are communities of either type a good thing?

First, some thoughts about the slippery notion of community itself. The term is sometimes used in a purely descriptive sense to name a grouping of persons with some degree of organization or a shared, recognized status. Thus we speak of "the medical community," "the law enforcement community," even "the explosives community" (Royal, 1995). Particular institutions can be communities in this sense: "the McCormack School community," "The University of Iowa community," "the Biogen Corporation community." In *this* sense an (ethnic) identity group *does* always constitute a community—a classificatory community ("the community of African Americans at the University of Massachusetts at Boston," for example).

"Community" in this descriptive sense contrasts with community in a valorized sense, in which the community (in the descriptive sense) is taken to realize some positive *value*, and not simply to exist as a social entity or classificatory group. Having a "*sense* of community" is a major way in which a community (in the descriptive sense) can realize a value. A neighborhood or school may entirely lack a sense of community in this sense. But the descriptive use may also be *aspirational*, implying an as-yet-unrealized potential for the achievement of a sense of community.

Yet not all communities with a sense of community are good or valuable communities. Nazi youth groups and religious cults often have a strong sense of community, yet they do not or may not realize positive values. A sense of community is no guarantee that the community (in the descriptive sense) is a good one, all told. It must also serve good, or at least non-objectionable, ends. A sense of community may be a good feature of a group that possesses other negative features, such as being loud and obnoxious, for example. Yet if a group crosses some threshold of "badness," we may no longer accord *any* value to its sense of community. For instance, a neo-Nazi group's strong sense of community would not normally be regarded as good, because it is so deeply implicated in the group's badness. In the case of educational institutions, we may assume that most at least aspire to serve genuinely good ends—the moral and intellectual growth of individuals, the preparation of informed citizens; hence a sense of community in them will be a good thing.

The contemporary movement known as "communitarianism" has contributed much to a revival of concern for community in the valorized sense (Etzioni, 1995; Sandel, 1982; Selznick, 1992). That movement has generally portrayed community in terms of a group of people—often based in a shared location, such as a neighborhood, but sometimes on a tradition (such as a religious one)—bound together by shared meanings or *shared values*. Should a neighborhood be able to exclude a pornographic bookstore? Should a St. Patrick's Day parade associated with South Boston be allowed to exclude an openly gay Irish group from participating, on the grounds that homosexuality is antithetical to the values of the South Boston community? These questions are raised by the "shared values" conception of community.

But sharing values is not sufficient for the sense of community at stake in the multiculturalism debates, in either inter- or intra-ethnic communities. For example, a multi-ethnic school with an intense culture of individual competitiveness and achievement, recognized and accepted as such by its staff and students, would be a community in the "shared values" sense. So would a school in which a strong sense of discipline and adherence to rules was accepted and valued. Yet neither school would necessarily embody the sense of common bond and attachment to other members presupposed in the "sense of community" that multiculturalists wish, or assume, in ethno-racial groups, and that pro-community anti-multiculturalists seek in classes, schools, and nations. Shared values can be "anti-communal" ones, yet they are still shared, and they can help define a community. But it will not be the kind of community generally desired in intra- and inter-ethnic communities. It will not have a "sense of community" in the required sense.

Some degree of shared values may be required for any community in the evaluative sense. However, the kinds of intra- or inter-ethnic communities I envision do not require that the students all have the same values in any general sense. It allows, and celebrates, the fact that children will bring many differences, including differences of values, to the school and the classroom. People can care for and care about those whose values differ from their own, and the pluralistic communities that constitute our schools in a culturally diverse society can attain a strong and overarching sense of "shared values" only at the cost of the recognition of their diversity. What may be correct, however, about the communitarian notion of shared values is that in order to be communities, the students must share certain values *with regard to the school setting itself*—values defining how people are to be treated, valuing of the school itself as an institution, and the like. But this leaves room for differing values about many other matters.

A sense of community, then, is not the same as (though it may involve) shared values. But what is a "sense of community," then? The term is too imprecise to find a single distinct answer. Let me suggest, then, at least *three* types of "sense of community" that can plausibly lay claim to this label. Each involves a somewhat distinct form of the human bond that connects the members of the community. Only one of these forms involves "caring" in the full sense in which it is used in the relevant literature; I will argue that this form is, when everything else is equal, the highest of the three forms of community. Nevertheless, individual caring in its own right lacks a type of collective or communal good possessed by the other two forms of community.

I will describe these ethno-racial communities primarily in the context of "visible" ethno-racial communities on school and college campuses. So I am here envisioning members of the same ethno-racial group who socialize (though not necessarily exclusively) with one another, eat together in the dining halls (at least some of the time), and are a distinct presence in the eyes of other students as members of that group; they may or may not be part of formal ethno-racial organizations.

Like the typology of ethnic identities, the following are ideal types. Actual communities may only approximately exemplify the values discussed, and may also embody more than one of the three values.

Belonging and Comfort

Communities may provide a sense of belonging and security, comfort and familiarity, to their members. Intra-ethnic groups on colleges are often experienced this way—a place or grouping to which members of a minority group who may not feel entirely comfortable in the larger institution can retreat for human sustenance among people with whom they feel comfortable, secure, and familiar. Stephen Carter (1993) describes the "black table," a place in the dining room of Yale Law School where black law students would gather at mealtimes to discuss issues of concern to them, where they could acknowledge their shared difference(s) from other students and proceed from that shared understanding.

Perhaps a "comfort" community is best realized among thickly ethnic students, as they have the most in common with regard to the ethno-racial dimension of their lives. Nevertheless, thin and identity ethnics may also experience this sense of comfort, though their sense of community will not replicate their home form of ethnic community. In fact, as mentioned earlier, residential colleges are often the first setting that identity ethnics experience themselves *as* ethnic, and they may feel a common bond and a desire, one they have never felt before, to socialize with fellow ethnics.

As I have described them, *pure* "anti-discrimination ethnics" are not likely to be members of comfort communities. They do not particularly desire to socialize with co-ethnics, nor necessarily feel any degree of personal comfort or familiarity with them.

The sense of comfort and security can not be generated by the mere co-presence of members of ethnic groups, of the thick, thin, and identity varieties. Personal and other factors may keep a collection of co-ethnics from "gelling" into a security community; they might, for example, just not hit it off with each other personally.

Solidarity and Loyalty to the Group

I conceive of *loyalty* and *solidarity* as involving a stronger sense of being bound up together, as having a "shared fate," than what is required by the security/comfort notion of community. Loyalty and solidarity require the members to stick up for one another and to join with one another in the face of outside threat or obstacle. By contrast, members of a comfort community could be something like fair-weather friends. They might feel comfortable with one another and have a sense of belonging and enjoy being with each other. But when all or some of its members encounter adversity, the group as a whole may not be counted on to stick together.

The community of solidarity is not merely a subgroup of the community of comfort. The solidarity community may include non-members of the comfort community, such as antidiscrimination ethnics who do not experience their ethno-racial group as a social comfort and familiarity group but may be there when the group is victimized. They do strongly identify with the group, but the tie is one of solidarity and loyalty rather than comfort. Of course, many students will feel *both* solidarity *and* comfort/security in the visible ethnic group. (Solidarity and loyalty may be directed to the wider classificatory ethnic community as well.)

While antidiscrimination ethnics feel loyalty and solidarity with their group, not all members of the loyalty community have an antidiscrimination consciousness. Loyalty untempered with justice (of which antidiscrimination is one form) is different from loyalty tempered with justice. The latter is exemplified by the antidiscrimination ethnic whose conviction that the group has genuinely suffered an injustice is a condition of her expressing solidarity; while the "pure" loyalty member simply sticks to and stands up for the group come what may. (In practice it is not always easy to distinguish these two types.) If, for example, the group has a clash of interest with some other group over resources for their respective student organizations, the antidiscrimination ethnic will not stand with her group if she does not feel they are being discriminated against with regard to the resource dispute, while the loyalty ethnic will. This is why a loyalty community, untempered by a sense of justice, is subject to a group egoism which diminishes the group's value; though, providing that the group is not dedicated to positively evil ends, I would still regard the loyalty as at least a limited virtue in that group.

Mutual Caring

A third kind of valorized community is characterized by mutual care and an intensified sense of individual responsibility of each for each other's welfare. While there are hints and seeds of this caring in the two previous forms of community, the more developed caring—the individualized caring described most fully by Nel Noddings (1984, 1992), and discussed and presupposed in much feminist and "carist" moral philosophy—is not guaranteed by either a comfort community or a loyalty community. To like to be with others, to feel comfortable with them, to share a culture with them, to feel socially secure with them—none of these requires or guarantees individualized attentiveness and concern for the welfare of the other members in the "mutual caring" community. However, all provide psychic and social contexts in which that caring can develop.

Similarly, the sense of solidarity involved in the loyalty community does not involve (or guarantee) this individualized attentiveness, either. Pulling together with, or joining, a group of one's co-ethnics in time of unjust treatment, and feeling a strong sense of solidarity with them, is by no means the same as knowing them individually, caring about them individually, and being concerned about the welfare of each individual.

To be sure, solidarity can be regarded as a *form* of caring. One would not stand with one's fellow ethnics unless one cared for them in *some* sense. For that matter, comfort/security/belonging involve a (different) form of care—(at least) a well-wishing, a pleasure in their pleasure. However, neither involves the type of care described by Noddings, the type rightly conceived of as grounding an "ethic of care," with its more intensified attentiveness to the other individual and her needs, her distinct personality, her way of viewing things, and the like.

The caring community in this sense is difficult to realize fully in any grouping of a fairly large number of persons; it is not possible to care in the Noddings sense for very many people at a given time—certainly only for fewer than those with whom one can feel either comfort or solidarity. Still, the caring community holds out an ideal which can be approximated to a greater or lesser extent among visible ethno-racial communities.

Aristotle's discussion of friendship provides a useful analogy here. He describes three types of friendship—pleasure, use, and character. All are genuine forms of friendship; they are not less than friendship. Yet only in character friendship is the other person truly loved for her own sake. In "pleasure" friendship, one enjoys the other's company and wishes her well, but does not love her for her own sake. The pleasure friendship is somewhat analogous to the "comfort community." (But the "use" friendship is *not* analogous to the solidarity community; the latter has no counterpart in Aristotle's scheme.) The character friendship is analogous to the caring community, in containing a higher degree of a characteristic important to all friendships (caring for the friend—analogous to the sense of bond with co-ethnics in communities).

Bonds of individualized care can grow up among fellow ethnics of all four kinds—thin, thick, identity (excepting type 1), and antidiscrimination. Temperament, interest, opportunity, and character of the individual will affect with whom these carings develop. But people can also work at caring for others, and a particular visible ethno-racial group on a given campus may have a culture or ethos that encourages the development of individualized caring, rather than, say, leaving the character of the community at the security/comfort stage.

CARING AND COLLECTIVITY

From the point of view of concern for individual welfare, caring communities are a more desirable—a "higher"—form of community than solidarity or comfort/security communities. The bonds between the members are stronger and deeper than in those other communities.

Nevertheless, the idea of individual attentive caring that informs a caring community does not capture the full range of value that people seek in communities, and, specifically, that students may seek in an ethnicity-based community in school or college. In particular, this caring does not necessarily guarantee a sense of *collectivity* that students from campus ethno-racial minority groups often expect and want.

Generally, ethnicity-based groups are not, or are not only, analogous to one's set of friends, each of whom one cares for individually, but who do not (necessarily) constitute a distinct, mutually recognizing group. Rather, the visible ethnic community thinks of itself as a distinct group, defined by shared ethnicity, within which the ties of friendship and care develop. As such, a collectivity can have an identity that is not reducible to the mere set of its members. Thus it can have interests, can view itself in relation to other groups, can feel itself under threat as a group. Some members may come to feel that the group is defining its ethnic identity in an unacceptable way—perhaps too narrow, or too nationalist, or too embracing of homophobia—or (in a different direction) too tepid or thin. In this case, some persons, even if they like and care for the individual members taking this group in (as they see it) an unfortunate direction, may choose to dissociate themselves from the group. This action, in turn, can threaten the identity and cohesion of the group as a whole—for example, by depriving it of a critical mass necessary for it even to be seen as a distinct ethnic group, or to experience itself as a distinct group, at that institution, in the visible sense.

The difference between pure *individual* caring, and the sense of collectivity involved in a caring (ethno-racial) community, involves the kinds of attitudes that the members have toward one another. For example, a member of the caring *community* is proud when a member of her group achieves something noteworthy; she sees this as reflecting on the group as a whole. She not only recognizes the other member's accomplishment and is *pleased* for her because she cares about her as a fellow student; she also feels pride *herself* because she identifies with the group and sees the other member's accomplishment as reflecting on the group.

Despite their weakness in guaranteeing a strong sense of mutual caring and responsibility, pure security communities *and* loyalty communities necessarily embody this collective dimension that individualized care does not. The familiarity, belonging, and security occur in relation to a distinct *group*, defined in terms of the shared characteristic of ethnicity, or ethnic identity, and a sense of collectivity built around that; the member's sense of security has its existence not only in relation to a random collection of individuals each of whom she feels secure with. Similarly, the loyalty involved in a loyalty community is directed not toward a mere collection of individual persons, but toward that *group*, when the group as a collectivity is threatened, insulted, or degraded. (It can also be generated by persecution of an individual; but it is the individual *as a member of the group*, as well as in her own right.) Perhaps the loyal member would *also* be loyal to individual members *purely* as individuals (e.g., as friends), but that is a different matter.

But could it not be replied that *caring* can itself be directed toward collectivities, as well as toward individuals, so the distinction I am attempting to draw really carries no weight? We can care that the group retains its integrity, that it stands for worthy ideals, that it engages in productive activities. We can embrace the notion of collectivity in our caring.

As Noddings points out, we can care for entities other than people— animals, the earth, ideas. These forms of caring differ in important ways from caring for individual persons. If the notion of care expands to include every form of appropriate moral relationship with every sort of entity warranting moral concern, the distinct individualized focus, the role of responsiveness of the other in caring, its operation independent of the formal demands of institutionalized structures and roles—all of which make the notion of care such a powerful moral conception and distinguish it so clearly from other moral conceptions (e.g., ones rooted in duty, obligation, pure rationality)—would be lost. The paradigm use of care should remain tied to caring for the other as a distinct *individual*. Independent of the terminological point of how broadly to employ the term *care*, the psychic operation of individualized person-to-person caring is distinct from that of attitudes toward collectivities, or toward individuals-as-members-of-collectivities.

So a caring *community* must be more than a group of individuals caring for one another individually in the fullest sense. It must embody a sense of ethno-racial collectivity, and the virtues that can attend it (such as concern and loyalty for the group). The individualized caring needs supplementing by collectivity-related values. (They may also need to be supplemented by justice, but that is another matter).

INTRA-ETHNIC AND INTER-ETHNIC COMMUNITIES: SOME IMPLICATIONS

While no claim of exhaustiveness can be made for this threefold typology of ethnicity-based communities and some of the values they are able to realize, it does suggest that there can be no *general* answer to the question, What is the value of ethnic communities? The answer depends on the values realized by particular communities. Similarly, there is no general answer to the question whether intra-ethnic communities detract from valuable inter-ethnic communities. That depends on the character of the ethnic community (as well as of the inter-ethnic one).

Some kinds of intra-ethnic communities detract from trans-ethnic ones much more than do others. Let us imagine two "ideal types" of security community (most college ethnic communities will be combinations of elements of both, but it is useful to consider the extremes). One consists of members who derive security and comfort from the ethno-community but are fearful, distrustful, and hostile to out-group members. They may see themselves as constantly victimized by other groups, or they may just be fearful of people who are different or who seem more able than they to negotiate the dominant culture of the educational institution.

The second ideal type of security community is one in which the members are bound by the comfort that stems from a shared culture (thin or thick, or something in between), but they are not negative toward or fearful of the wider multi-ethnic community. The members all have friends from other groups, participate in activities that bridge different groups, and evince loyalty to and concern for the larger institution by playing on sports teams and involving themselves in (multi-ethnic) service projects, various levels of student government, and the like. Perhaps they more frequently sit with fellow ethnics in dining rooms or cafeterias than with others. But they do not *always* do so, and they feel entirely comfortable in many multi-ethnic settings.

I am asserting, without distinct empirical support, that the less exclusivist comfort community can provide as strong a sense of comfort/belonging/security as the more exclusivist one. But some research does suggest that non-exclusivist ethno-racial identities are healthier forms of ethno-racial identity than exclusivist ones (see Tatum, 1996).

Obviously the fearful/hostile ethnic community is much more inimical to trans-ethnic community than is the accepting/expansive one. The former's members will be poor candidates for attempts to forge cross-ethnic ties and to generate a loyalty to the institution itself, or at least a loyalty experienced as gladly shared with members of other groups. It does not follow, however, that the mere *existence* of the fearful visible ethnic community, and of organizations and practices through which it is realized, *by itself* detracts from the development of wider ethno-racial ties and community. It could be that without the ethnicity-based community, the particular members of the ethnic group in question would be alienated equally from the larger community. They simply would not have *any* community in which they were comfortable. Merely depriving students of the option of an ethnicity-based communal attachment and recognition does not by itself promote wider cross-ethnic attachments and loyalties, as some anti-multiculturalism seems to presume. The existence of such organizations does not prevent, nor does its absence guarantee, trans-ethnic communities.

CONCLUSION

I have argued that there are at least four importantly distinct types of ethnicity: two kinds of ethno/racial identity (thick and thin), identity (with three subgroups), and antidiscrimination (an instance of one of the subdivisions of identity ethnicity). Ethno-racial identity can have quite different meanings for different people. The typology allows us to recognize the distinction between ethno-culture and ethnic identity; not everyone who possesses an ethnic identity that can be personally significant necessarily partakes of its corresponding ethno-culture(s).

At the same time, shared ethnic identity in any of its forms is no guarantee of a substantial sense of *community* with fellow ethnics, in an educational (or other) institution. (*Culture, identity,* and *community* are more distinct from one another than writings on multiculturalism often presuppose.) Nevertheless, institutionally visible ethnic communities can readily encompass all four types of ethnic identity.

I have argued that different sorts of community realize different values. I have distinguished among security/comfort/belonging, loyalty/solidarity, and mutual (individualized) care as distinct values realized by different kinds of ethnic communities. A sense of collectivity, present in both the security and loyalty communities, must complement the individual care of the caring community in order to realize something close to a full range of values realizable by intra-ethnic communities.

The group-based goods of security, belonging, loyalty, and solidarity that ethno-racial groups can realize are thus distinct from the values of individual caring. They are also distinct from justice, and can, but by no means must, come in conflict with it.

Finally, I have briefly suggested how this analysis helps us see that the relations between intra-ethnic communities and trans-ethnic communities (in shared institutions) must be varied and complex. It is not simply a matter of choosing between one and the other, as anti-multiculturalists, on one side, and cultural chauvinists and nationalists, on the other, generally assume. A next step would be to examine the character of inter-ethnic communities. Only then would we be in a position to address the question of relations between the two.

Acknowledgments. I wish to thank Benjamin Blum-Smith and Marcia Homiak for very helpful comments on drafts of this article.

REFERENCES

Appiah, K. Anthony. (1996). Culture, subculture, multiculturalism: Educational options. In R. Fullinwider (Ed.), *Public education in a multicultural society: Policy, theory, critique* (pp. 65–89). New York: Cambridge University Press.

Blum, Lawrence. (1994). Gilligan's two voices and the moral status of group identity. In Lawrence Blum, *Moral perception and particularity*. New York: Cambridge University Press.

Carter, Stephen. (1993). The black table, the empty seat, and the tie. In Gerald Early (Ed.), *Lure and loathing: Essays on race, identity, and the ambivalence of assimilation* (pp. 55–79). New York: Penguin Books.

Etzioni, Amitai. (Ed.). (1995). *New communitarian thinking: Persons, virtues, institutions, and communities*. Charlottesville: University Press of Virginia.

Gans, Herbert. (1996). Symbolic ethnicity: The future of ethnic groups and cultures in America. In Werner Sollors (Ed.), *Theories of ethnicity: A classical reader* (pp. 425–459). New York: New York University Press.

Hacker, Andrew. (1995). *Two nations: Black and white, separate, hostile, unequal* (2nd ed.). New York: Ballantine Books.

Hollinger, David. (1995). *Postethnic America: Beyond multiculturalism*. New York: Basic Books.

Kaye-Kantrowitz, Melanie. (1996). Jews in the USA: The costs of whiteness. In B. Thompson & S. Tyagi (Eds.), *Names we call home* (pp. 121–138). New York: Routledge.

Navarrette, Ruben, Jr. (1993). *A darker shade of crimson: Odyssey of a Harvard Chicano*. New York: Bantam.

Noddings, Nel. (1984). *Caring: A feminine approach to ethics and moral education*. Berkeley: University of California Press.

Noddings, Nel. (1992). *The challenge to care in schools*. New York: Teachers College Press.

Royal, Robert. (1995). Introduction: Restoring self-governing community. In R. Royal (Ed.). *Reinventing the American people: Unity and diversity today* (pp. 1–18). Grand Rapids, MI: William Eerdmans Publishing Co.

Sandel, Michael. (1982). *Liberalism and the limits of justice*. New York: Cambridge University Press.

Scott, Joan. (1995). Multiculturalism and the politics of identity. In John Rajchman (Ed.), *The identity in question* (pp. 3–14). New York: Routledge.

Selznick, Philip. (1992). *The moral commonwealth: Social theory and the promise of community*. Berkeley: University of California Press.

Tatum, Beverly Daniel. (1996). Talking about race, learning about racism: The application of racial identity development theory in the classroom. In T. Beauboeuf-Lafontant & D. Smith Augustine (Eds.), *Facing racism in education* (2nd ed.; pp. 321–348). Cambridge, MA: Harvard Educational Review.

Waters, Mary. (1990). *Ethnic options: Choosing identities in America*. Berkeley: University of California Press.

CHAPTER 9

School Sexual Harassment Policies: The Need for Both Justice and Care

Elizabeth Chamberlain
and
Barbara Houston

> Sexual harassment in school is the worst. . . . As a girl you can't be accepted unless you wear big clothes. Then it's like, "Oh, a girl," not like, "Oh, a body."
> (Orenstein, 1994, p. 262)

We are all familiar with the fact, if only from our own experience, that a certain level of sexual teasing happens in school. But we may not be aware that it characterizes the daily lives of some students. We may not know the extent of sexual bullying and humiliation that occurs, nor the serious harm associated with it.

There is now ample evidence that student-to-student harassment exists, and that it adversely affects students educationally, socially, and emotionally (Larkin, 1994; Sherer, 1994; Shoop & Edwards, 1994; Stein & Sjostrom, 1994; J. Strauss, 1993; S. Strauss, 1992). In 1993, the American Association of University Women (AAUW) sponsored a large-scale survey of students in grades 8 to 11 in which 85 percent of the girls and 76 percent of the boys reported having been sexually harassed at school, with most students reporting the first instance of sexual harassment having happened between grades 6 and 9. In this same survey girls overwhelmingly reported that they subsequently experienced serious consequences from being sexually harassed, including a reluctance to attend school, more frequent absences, a decision to remain silent in classes, difficulty in paying attention, studying, or working on projects at school, and a change of educational plans and vocational aspirations to avoid other likely occasions of harassment (AAUW, 1993).

The law has addressed sexual harassment both in the workplace and in schools. Legally oriented policies which define and prohibit sexual harassment are in place in public schools. Still, student-to-student sexual harassment remains ubiquitous (Shoop & Edwards, 1994; Stein & Sjostrom, 1994; Streitmatter, 1994). The policies seem not to work. Girls do not use them and do not trust them (Stein, 1993; S. Strauss, 1992). The question is why?

It is our view that the policies do not work because schools treat sexual harassment as a legal issue rather than as an educational issue which has legal components. Court cases have been useful in making schools aware of student-to-student sexual harassment, but they have also led schools to frame the problem almost exclusively as a legal issue, to be handled bureaucratically, not as an educational issue that demands pedagogical attention.

In this chapter we briefly trace the development of legally oriented school sexual harassment policies and note their shortcomings. We call the school policies on sexual harassment legally oriented because they reflect case law, they use legal terms and definitions in their formulation, and the primary impetus for writing the policies has often been to avoid legal liability. Such policies are thought to operationalize justice in the school setting by focusing on rights and procedures. They grant students both the power to name sexual harassment as a wrong, and the right to claim redress. We contend that such an approach, while helpful, is by itself inadequate. We argue that an effective student-to-student sexual harassment policy must acknowledge the developmental level of students to whom the policy applies; the complex social system in which students function; the local cultural norms which tend to override the legal dictates; and the unequal social standing among students. We go on to develop the view that policies more appropriate to schools which aim to provide a framework for education and growth, and not merely for restriction and punitive controls, will require a deliberate education oriented meshing of a justice/rights framework with that of the ethics of care.

For several reasons we focus our discussion on male-to-female student harassment in public coeducational middle schools. (Although we have chosen to use the terms *middle school* and *middle school students*, we mean to include all those who might be called "middle level students," i.e., students who attend either or both middle school and junior high school.)

First, a lot of student-to-student sexual harassment happens in these venues. The middle school is the site of the marked escalation of sexual harassment within the public educational system (Stein, 1993). Second, along with other researchers and educators, we are concerned with an array of "symptoms" that show up among early adolescent women: a silencing of their voices (Gilligan, Lyons, & Hammer, 1990), a drop in self-esteem (AAUW, 1993; Orenstein, 1994), a loss of academic achievement, and a diminished sense of personal direction (AAUW, 1993; Fine, 1993), along with the onslaught of problems such as eating disorders, depression, and self-mutilation (Pipher, 1994). These are precisely the reactions female adolescents report as their response to their experiences of chronic pervasive sexual harassment, especially in middle school settings (Larkin, 1994; Stein & Sjostrom, 1994; S. Strauss, 1992). Our third reason for focusing on the middle school is that we have an obvious ethical responsibility to serve as models, protectors, guides, and advisors to these students, and they have ethical potential to make use of that guidance. Students at this age are for the most part open to ethical reflection about sexual harassment and still anticipate that adults will provide boundaries and guidelines for them. In order to satisfy that responsibility, however, we need to be sure which policies will best express our values.

Two preliminary observations: first, it is common to call student-to-student sexual harassment "peer harassment," but for reasons which will become evident later, we find the latter term misleading and prefer the former. Second, it seems to us that the voices and stories of students are most effective in illuminating the situations students experience. Consequently, we use examples drawn from published ethnographies as well as representative composites from contributor Elizabeth Chamberlain's 20 years of experience in middle schools.

THE LAW AND SCHOOL SEXUAL HARASSMENT POLICIES

There is no doubt that the legal recognition and definition of sexual harassment has been the impetus for educators to grapple with the phenomena in public school settings. Explicit legal procedures and clarification of key terms have raised the awareness of both students and staff to the seriousness of the matter.

In response to legal developments, various manuals, guides, and publications have been written, designed to assist school administrators and faculty in formulating policies which will be legally viable. The definition of sexual harassment typically echoes the languages and policies established in adult workplaces. For example, one current student handbook version reads:

> Sexual harassment means unwanted sexual advances, requests for sexual favors, and other inappropriate verbal, written, or physical conduct of a sexual nature. Such behavior can interfere with performance and can create an intimidating or offensive environment. Some examples of sexual harassment include: subtle pressure for sexual activity; unwelcome touching or other physical contact (inappropriate intimacy, grabbing/touching/shoving/groping/rubbing-up-against/ cornering); spreading sexual rumors, including graffiti; sexist remarks about an individual's clothing, ability, body, or sexual activity; teasing about bodily functions, stage of physical development, or one's sex in general; gestures, jokes, pictures, leers. (Oyster River Cooperative School District Policy, 1994, p. 6)

These legally oriented school policies make a strong positive contribution to the mitigation of sexual harassment in two important ways. First, by naming, providing definitions, and making legally actionable many insidious behaviors which have hitherto been discomforting, embarrassing, and offensive, yet not legally identifiable, they give validation and importance to the perceptions of those who have endured such behaviors and they make available a sanctioned platform from which to discuss them. Second, legally oriented policies have made it clear that the power to determine that an action is discomforting or unwanted rests with the one receiving the action, regardless of the actor's tacit or stated intentions. For vulnerable persons, this is a significant shift in determining who controls access to one's person. Regardless of whether the objectionable action is a verbal comment, a gesture, a look, or a touch, the receiver of the action determines its acceptability.

Most significant, the legal characterization of sexual harassment confers rights on those targeted in sexual harassment: the right to define and defend one's own personal space, the right to limit access to one's body and clothing, the right to proclaim one's feelings of violation, and the right to defend one's reputation against sexual rumors or graffiti—in short, the right to be treated with respect, not as a sexual object.

Obviously, legally oriented policies are not insignificant. As Catharine MacKinnon (1987) observes, "The law is not everything—but it is not nothing, either" (p. 116). Useful as it is to see legally oriented sexual harassment policies as rights granting, it is important to avoid two implausible reductionistic tendencies—to equate legal policy with justice, and to interpret justice solely in terms of the assertion and reinforcement of rights. It would be a mistake to reject or undervalue legally oriented policies; it would, however, also be a mistake to think that such policies are enough. In our view they are from an educational perspective insufficient, and from an ethical perspective unsatisfactory.

THE SHORTCOMINGS OF LEGALLY ORIENTED POLICIES

While legally oriented sexual harassment policies may conceivably protect a school district from liability, there is little if any evidence that such policies prevent or even interrupt the incidence of student-to-student sexual harassment in public schools. In fact, reports indicate not only that has student-to-student harassment continued unabated, but that students distrust the policies and are reluctant to use them (J. Strauss, 1993; Stein, 1993). This leads us to ask exactly why these policies fail to alter the patterns of sexual harassment in middle schools. What prevents girls from accessing the procedures that are in place to empower them to both name the offense and claim their rights?

One serious substantive shortcoming of the policies, from our point of view, is the mismatch between the legal categories of sexual harassment and its occurrence in the middle school milieu. Two specific problems emerge when the legal categories of sexual harassment defined by the court, either "quid pro quo" or "hostile environment," are employed in sexual harassment policies for middle schools. First, the categories fail to cover what, from an educational point of view, we would regard as significant harm; and second, this dichotomous characterization of sexual harassment leaves student-to-student harassment covered by the more ambiguous category, "hostile environment." The latter category is confusing for administrators, teachers, and students, and it also requires too high a threshold of harm before intervention is warranted.

Of the two forms of sexual harassment the law recognizes, "quid pro quo" and "hostile environment," the former means literally "something for something." It applies only in instances where one person is in a formally recognized position of power or authority over another and (1) uses that position to exert pressure for sexual favors or (2) engages in sexual conversations, gestures, or comments to someone who has formally less authority, or alternatively, (3) retaliates for the latter's refusal of sexual advances. While it would appear that this category might adequately cover teacher-to-student sexual harassment, there are only certain losses the court recognizes—for example, diminishment of a grade, or poor letters of reference. It will not cover such losses as lowering of self-esteem, or diminishment of comfort level, social status, or emotional well-being which the receiver of sexual harassment may experience and which, from an educational point of view, can be potentially devastating and cause developmental harms.

The court's dichotomous characterization of sexual harassment means that by default all student-to-student harassment falls into the "hostile environment" category because students are considered peers (i.e., of equal formal standing within the school). However, as Shoop & Edwards (1994) point out, the determination of "hostile environment" is confusing for educators because the behavior can occur over a period of time and include a large variety of incidents and possibly a large number of actors. In cases of "hostile environment," a plethora of comments, activities, insinuations, and practice may combine to create a general atmosphere which does not respect females as a gender, yet no one specific actor is easily seen to be accountable for the continuation or creation of that "hostile environment." And it may not be clear to any of the actors or officials that such behavior exceeds the norm and alters conditions to the point where they can be deemed "hostile." Thus this category too fails to cover straightforwardly behavior that makes students feel insulted or uneasy (and causing them to report, "I never go down that hallway" or "I don't eat lunch at noon because they're there" or "I won't take classes if he's going to be in them").

We suggest that the legal categories and legally oriented policies are too blunt to be the sole or primary instrument used to deal with student-to-student harassment in educational settings. In particular, with student-to-student harassment, when the legal template is applied, too much of what we need to attend to falls outside its jurisdiction. And unfortunately, once a school has a legally oriented policy in place, the tendency is to think that only behavior which clearly satisfies the standard of proof required by law is worthy of educators' attention.

But the far more serious difficulty with the current legally oriented approach is the assumption of school policy makers that information about its illegality and the available enforcement of rights are sufficient to reduce the incidence of sexual harassment.

The alarming and disheartening finding is that these policies do very little to reduce student-to-student sexual harassment because (1) administrators, teachers, and students do not recognize student-to-student sexual harassment when it occurs (i.e., they can't name it as such); and (2) even when they do recognize it, research tells us that many who suffer it are reluctant to claim redress (Larkin, 1994; Mann, 1994; Stein & Sjostrom, 1994; J. Strauss, 1993).

Rather than blaming administrators for their ineptness in applying the policy or students for their hesitancy to use the policy and their mistrust of it, we think we can get further by investigating the assumptions of those who are content to rely solely on legally oriented policies. In particular, we need to examine two assumptions: (1) the Reconfiguration Presupposition—the assumption that students and staff will have no difficulty in naming "normal" patterns of behavior as inappropriate, wrong, or illegal; and (2) the Equality Presumption—that all student actors, male or female, have equal standing within social relationships (i.e., that all students have both the agency to act in their own behalf and community permission to do so). Sadly, both presumptions are highly questionable in middle school settings.

The Reconfiguration Presupposition: Naming the Offense

The assumption that legal definitions and lists of examples of forbidden behaviors are sufficient to allow staff and students to identify and eliminate sexual harassment in their schools takes for granted that there is a cultural consensus on naming what is "sexual," "offensive," and "unwelcome." But when we are dealing with sexual harassment among early adolescents in a middle school setting, the single most significant obstacle remarked on repeatedly by researchers is the difficulty staff and students have in distinguishing offensive behaviors such as those covered by sexual harassment policies from "normal heterosexual behavior" (Larkin, 1994; Shoop & Edwards, 1994; Stein & Sjostrom, 1994; J. Strauss, 1993).

The behaviors addressed by sexual harassment policies are inseparable from the entire web of social customs and encultured beliefs which define us as male and female. Much of the behavior which policies make "illegal" and wrong is often seen as normalized heterosexual behavior in the eyes of students and staff.

Middle school students and their teachers and parents are immersed in a larger culture in which sexual innuendo and sexualized comments are embedded in nearly all forms of media. Advertisements, television programs, music, video games, and even T-shirts present sexual images and messages in direct opposition to attitudes of mutual regard and respect between genders.

Socially insecure and with limited repertoires of behavior to use during courtship rituals of adolescence, both boys and girls may resort to crude or inept attempts to gain the attention of one another. Donna Eder (1995) in her ethnographic study of middle schools records numerous conversations between groups of girls and boys where the agenda was for a girl and a boy to establish that they are interested in "going with" one another. (It is a peculiar norm that such conversations among middle-level students generally do take place in groups, not individually.) Eder records examples of such group conversations disintegrating from awkward to vulgar in a matter of minutes.

Another source of confusion for many middle school students is the tendency to rely on an intention analysis when assessing one's own behavior, a practice not unknown to adults. In instances of sexually harassing behavior, people are apt to define or categorize their own behavior in terms of intention rather than the content or the consequences of the behavior. In daily social interactions intent does matter. One reacts differently to an inadvertent contact in a crowded elevator than to a purposeful shove. Yet a person's intent is difficult to document and not always relevant. In cases of sexual harassment, the intention of "being funny" or "having fun" on the part of the offender does not prevent a comment or action from being received as hurtful, offensive, intrusive, intimidating, or assaultive.

Individual interpretations influenced in large part by the surrounding cultural practices may vary greatly from the explicit legal definitions of proscribed behaviors which appear on a list in a policy statement. And the cultural normalization may be so widely accepted that no one within the cultural setting will be inclined to question or challenge local interpretation. To illustrate this point we offer the following example.

Bra snapping appears on nearly every list of prohibited behaviors in published sexual harassment policies, yet it remains nearly ubiquitous in middle school settings (AAUW, 1993; Stein, 1993; S. Strauss, 1992). One author has discussed this behavior with scores of young men and their parents, who appear to be at a loss to understand why anyone would classify what they perceive to be a harmless, playful "greeting" gesture as objectionable. Their confusion stems not from a lack of understanding about what bra snapping is, but from the context in which it is prohibited. Both students and parents know, for example, that it is not an acceptable greeting for a grandmother, an adult staff member, or a stranger at the shopping mall. Yet their interpretation of it as a way to say "Hi" or gain the momentary attention of a female classmate remains firm. Fathers often shake their heads and echo the students' viewpoint, saying, "I remember doing it at this age— everyone does." Mothers recall being subjected to it and also tend to accept it as a middle school phenomenon, one which may be classified as a mild annoyance or even as a positive sign of male interest.

The adult school staff may contribute to the confusion between the naming of an action and the cultural meaning that becomes ascribed to it. When teachers in a faculty training session on sexual harassment discussed bra snapping, there was consensus about what the behavior was and that it constituted violation of the person. Still, several staff indicated that if or when they witnessed it during the course of a class, they might not intercede (1) if the girl did not appear to object, or (2) if dealing with the action would create a major interruption of the class in progress.

Without entering a full discussion about consent, suffice it to note that a student may appear to be consenting to an action when she is not. The teacher's assessment based on a quick observation is insufficient to assess the quality or depth of consent. And when a girl knows that a teacher has witnessed an action such as bra snapping and does not intervene, the girl will have no confidence that her perception of being violated will be validated, and she may therefore continue to give passive obedience to the custom, assuming that her own perception of being unjustly discomforted is inaccurate. If a girl does protest under such circumstances, she may be cited for creating a class disruption (Eder, 1995; Larkin, 1994) or be ostracized by her peers for faulty social skills and an inability to interpret a male gesture accurately (Larkin, 1994). In short, the offended girl has no way to access the official sexual harassment policy without accepting negative consequences for herself. If, after a period of time, this student does complain that a specific male classmate has repeatedly snapped her bra and refused to stop after being requested to do so, and in effect, begins the legal process of filing a grievance, she is likely to be asked what took her so long to complain and come under suspicion herself as a co-contributor to the problem.

The point is that the definitions and procedures outlined in a sexual harassment policy are not only open to interpretations mediated by individuals' and groups' understanding of specific intentions and circumstances, they are also in direct opposition to the norms, values, and beliefs of a cultural setting when they define as offensive and objectionable the same behaviors that have been ritualized and condoned by local social practices. If students, and teachers, are successfully to reconfigure "normal" behavior as sexual harassment, we shall need to have recourse to a more complex and more subtle pedagogy than a statement of legal definitions accompanied by a listing of prohibited behaviors.

The Equality Presumption: Claiming Redress

The equality presumption is the name we give to the fact that legalistic policies are designed as a one-size-fits-all policy. Such policies ignore differences between adults in a workplace setting and youngsters in school settings; they also ignore the differences in social standing between females and males within the wider culture and within the middle school culture.

Unlike workplaces, schools are contexts we create for the explicit purpose of helping youngsters who are still growing to learn, change, and develop socially and emotionally as well as intellectually. Legally oriented sexual harassment policies fail to take into account the social developmental patterns we know occur with adolescents. For example, one of these developmental tasks is to test rules and explore boundaries established by adults. Whether discovering ingenious ways to chew gum in science class without detection or to insult a peer sexually, thus gaining a momentary feeling of power, the adolescent is busy playing what educators at this level dub the "stump-the-adult game."

Barrie Thorne (1994) and Donna Eder (1995), in their ethnographic studies of middle level schools, have documented many of the "games" in which young adolescents engage. Males, in particular, engage in contests among themselves. These demonstrations of "toughness" may include spitting contests, belching fests, or insult competitions. Eder points out that the boys were expected to demonstrate their masculinity by controlling their emotions during insult exchanges and that "keeping cool" during sexual insults posed the biggest challenge. The girls in Eder's study, however, did not engage in such insult games, and when they became targets of the boys' games, they had neither the practice to keep their cool nor the repertoire of insults to "play the game." The boys' comments to the girls clearly implied that they were viewing the girls as sexual objects and as convenient practice targets. The following scene happened in a lunchroom setting:

> Cindy came over to the table and wanted to know who was throwing stuff. She addressed herself to Eric. Eric grabbed her arms when she got close. Joe told her that he wanted to eat her and grabbed her waist. She told him to let go. Joe said he changed his mind and walked away. Eric started pulling her down on his lap and told her, "Just a little more. I can almost see down your shirt." She got away, and before she attacked Eric, Bobby called her over and started talking to her. She calmed down immediately. (Eder, 1995, p. 88)

As obvious as the sexual harassment is in this scene, neither Cindy nor the boys viewed it as such. They believed they were engaged in game behavior; Cindy did not enjoy the encounter, but she still accepted it as a game.

The point here is that one of the accepted differences between adults and youngsters is that the latter are still acquiring knowledge about what it means to show respect for persons and what counts as a violation of that respect. We can't assume they have that knowledge.

Ironically, the most important single virtue of a legally oriented policy is also its most significant defect: it assumes that students are peers and equals: each can be violated, and if violated, each can claim redress. This fails to acknowledge the prevailing power imbalance that exists between males and females, a fact which has a bearing both upon the ability to name sexual harassment as such, and, perhaps more significant, upon the ability to claim redress.

Any school policy which realistically hopes to address student-to-student harassment must acknowledge that the conventional norms of acceptable male sexual overtures or expressions reflect a system of male dominance that gives males unquestioned right of access to females (Frye, 1983; Rich, 1979). Rituals of courtship in the larger culture are characterized by male initiatives, including aggression, and assume that females both seek and desire such initiatives. Additionally, females are held accountable for dual and often conflicting duties of both attracting male attention and setting limits upon male behavior.

Student surveys on sexual harassment reported by Susan Strauss (1992) are revealing: from a group of males, "It's a man thing. When a girl has on something revealing, you have to say something about it. . . . If a girl doesn't tell us we're sexually harassing her, we're going to continue to do it" (pp. 15-17).

Another consequence of the fact that sexual harassment is part of a larger framework that constructs gender as a dominant-subordinate relation between boys and girls, men and women, is that the very notion of "victim" is problematic. While being acknowledged as a victim is supposed to be helpful in having others recognize that the target of sexual harassment did not cause, and is not responsible for, the rude actions of others and places legal responsibility on the actor who violated the rules, the target person still needs to develop a sense of her own agency to respond, to access the policy procedure for justice, and to claim her rights. But as Susan Wendell (1990) notes, "Victims can and frequently do take the perspective of the oppressor. The victim with this perspective usually feels guilty for her or his victimization and takes all or most of the responsibility for it" (p. 24).

In cases of sexual harassment, it has been our experience that all the parties affected—parents, staff, and other students—join the "victim" in continuing this stance of her accepting responsibility. "You shouldn't have worn that dress," "You shouldn't have teased him first," "You were obviously flaunting yourself in front of those guys," "What were you doing there?" and other similar pronouncements of the victim's culpability abound.

It can be especially hurtful when other students echo the blame-the-victim reaction. A girl reported to Orenstein (1994) that while managing the boys' basketball team, she had been grabbed:

And this boy Fred walked up during practice and he just reached out [she extended both arms] and he grabbed both of my tits. And this other boy standing there said, "Did he just touch you?" I said, "Yeah," and he said, "Fred, you shouldn't do that." Fred said, "I didn't do anything!" and walked away. Then this guy turns to me and says, "Next time, you really should watch yourself." Like it was my fault! (p. 262)

Such judgments create an environment where it becomes unlikely that the target of harassment will feel justified and supported in claiming her rights. She will not feel empowered to effect a change or develop a plan to change the prevailing customs of harassment: the only option which presents itself is for her to restrict *her own* movements, dress, and interactions.

In one of the middle schools Peggy Orenstein studied, a guidance counselor, hearing that sexual harassment was a problem for girls, convened a group to discuss what was happening. At first the girls were most reluctant to give specifics about behaviors directed at them or the names of the boys involved. Orenstein reports the full transcript of the meeting, and midway through the time allocated for the meeting she notes:

> The girls are loosening up now, and a tone of exasperation is replacing their initial reluctance. They begin recounting boys' remarks in detail: they talk about boys who say, "Suck my fat Peter, you slut," who call them "shank" and "ho" (a variation on "whore" popularized by male rap artists). They talk about boys who pinch their bottoms in the hallways or grab their breasts and shout, "Let me tune in Tokyo!" They insist it isn't just "bad" boys who badger them: it's boys with good grades, boys who are athletes, boys who are paragons of the school. *And they all agree, their fear of reprisal is much too acute to allow them to confront their harassers.* (p. 120; emphasis added)

No Means For Reconciliation

Social relationships are the essential purpose of life for most middle school students. Their reasons for attending school have less to do with compulsory attendance laws or educational aspirations than for making and maintaining their social relationships. Legally oriented policies on sexual harassment do not recognize the crucial importance of the maintenance of the social network which precedes, follows, and surrounds an occasion of sexual harassment. Most sexual harassment in schools occurs among classmates and friends. If, or when, a "victim" does claim her rights, she must manage to do so while maintaining daily relationships with the "perpetrator" and his friends, for unlike the circumstances in a case of being mugged by a stranger on the street, the target of an attack in school cannot avoid returning to the "scene of the crime." The need to maintain friendships, to be accepted by peers, and not to be labeled a snitch, a rat, or "the girl who got Bobby in trouble" often overrides the wish to defend oneself or one's rights.

Both the strain one experiences for snitching and the struggle to maintain relationships in spite of conflict surrounding a sexual harassment incident is apparent in this typical note sent by a girl to her "best friend," who had complained about a popular boy touching her (picture this written in fuschia marker, covering two full pages):

> Hey, Bitch—I don't know why you got Bobby in trouble. He is a really good kid. Now he's mad and is really going to beat your butt. I don't know why you did that—he's wicked cute. You better tell Ms. Chamberlain you made it up or we'll tell everyone that your[sic] a ho and what you did with Steve. Smarten up, bitch. [signed,] your best friend 4eva[sic] (please write back), Sally. P.S. Want to go to the mall after school? [with small boxes to be checked yes or no].

A female who resists or challenges the male's de facto right to embarrass, touch, or tease her risks rupturing relationships not only with the male(s) charged with harassment, but also with other females who are struggling to maintain heterosexual relationships.

One of us was poignantly reminded of this fact at the end of a counseling session with a group of girls who had had complaints about the way boys were treating them. The girls had been able to identify the sorts of actions that made them uncomfortable and had devised viable ways to confront harassers and strategies for resistance. At the end of the group session one of the girls commented: "In here, we're so strong—so sure of ourselves. But when we get back to class, we don't *do* the things we *plan* in here." Another student responded, "Yeah, because, you know, you have to be careful. I mean, you still have to have somebody to dance with."

SCHOOL SEXUAL HARASSMENT POLICIES, JUSTICE, AND CARE

Let us be clear. We are not claiming that the aforementioned difficulties of sexual harassment policies are difficulties of the law. Rather, the mistake, we have argued, is to think that sole reliance on legally oriented policies can be educationally sufficient. From an ethical perspective, it may be accurate to say that justice and rights are *implicit* in legally oriented sexual harassment policies, but they are difficult to activate.

From an educational perspective, students' confusions about rights range widely. Some express bewilderment even about how to conduct conversations with one another when they have become conscious of respecting rights. One boy who had been disciplined for sexually harassing a female classmate expressed his confusion about what to him were new and strange rules. He told Peggy Orenstein (1994), "I'll just wait until high school, and talk to girls then" (p. 128). At the other, more dangerous extreme, Michelle Fine and Pat Macpherson (1992) report that some adolescent women, in order to conform to the prevailing social order, accepted constriction on their person rights, including the right to be free of sexual assault from their boyfriends. They were aware of the existence of their rights in the abstract but could not envision a heterosexual relationship that would, or could, accommodate the enactment of their rights.

Such difficulties should not dissuade us from having justice and rights be a goal, something we pursue, but we do need to recognize that we can hit a barrier when the social nexus, the relationships presupposed by rights, does not support the stated policy. What is genuinely problematic is not the adoption of policies which acknowledge rights but rather the absence of what Minow (1990) calls "the only precondition" for the exercise of one's rights, namely, "that the community be willing for the individual to make claims and to participate in the defining and redefining of personal and social boundaries" (p. 301).

An Ethics of Care Perspective

One way to deal with this barrier is to bring in another ethical perspective, one that focuses on relationships as does the ethics of care (Gilligan, 1982; Noddings, 1984, 1992), whose fundamental imperative instructs us to maintain and enhance caring relations—that is, relations marked by "a commitment to receptive attention and a willingness to respond helpfully to legitimate needs" (Noddings, 1996, p. 265). There are several ways in which the introduction of a care perspective can assist us in developing more ethically satisfying and educationally effective sexual harassment policies.

First, the ethics of care would have us pay greater attention to the *particularities* of the persons and situations for which school sexual harassment policies are designed: more attention to *what* we are trying to accomplish, and *how*, for *whom*, in what *setting*, and with what *attitude*. It would prompt us to notice that we are dealing with youngsters who are in the midst of their social development, who are still learning how to be with others, how to establish relationships with others. Further, it would have us pay attention to the fact that we are discussing policies for adolescents in *schools*; that is, in a context in which one expects mistakes and subsequent learning from them, in social institutions which are or ought to be committed to educating students even about caring relations. This means that coercion may not be ruled out, but we will want to make sure that any coercion we invoke is not exercised in a manner that contradicts caring (Noddings, 1990).

Second, the ethics of care better explains some of the students' difficulties with sexual harassment policies. When girls resist using the formal procedures available to them to name a wrong and seek redress, when they are hesitant to exercise their rights because they "don't want to make trouble for him," or because they still want to "have someone to dance with," they may well be caught in what from the ethics of care perspective we can recognize as an *ethical* dilemma. On one hand, they want to care for themselves and resist their violation, on the other, they feel the obligations of friendship and do not want to rupture valued relationships with peers. If we fully appreciate their dilemma as an ethical one, involving competing moral values, we are more likely to be moved to change the conditions that place them in conflict rather than construe the situation as one in which female students simply lack the interest, skill, or courage needed to assert their rights.

Once we take seriously the ethics of care's imperative to maintain and enhance caring relations, and we see how we might foster more caring as well as just relations among students, we can appreciate that the ethics of care has one great advantage over an approach that focuses only on justice and rights: it affords us a way to begin the work of reconciliation among the students, when appropriate. The practice of care can help us to differentiate cases—between those offenders who say, "If I had known it would have such bad consequences for her, I wouldn't have done it," and those visible offenders who are well-known, defiant repeaters. For the latter, coercion and the full demands of justice, along with re-education efforts, are needed to ensure the safety of the school community. For the former, we can begin to see their "crimes" as conflicts between students, an impairment of their relations that more appropriately might call for reconciliation rather than punishment and retribution (Knopp, 1991). Understanding the conflict within the larger communal context of the classroom and the school community, we can begin to look at how we can establish, or reestablish, trust and trustworthiness, and restore mutual caring relations. A care perspective might encourage what we could call "restorative justice" (Knopp, 1991, p. 183).

Another consequence of introducing an ethics of care perspective into our discussion of school sexual harassment policies is that we can gain a different perspective upon rights. The ethics of care has us recognize that rights are grounded in the process of communication and meaning making rather than in some abstract legal foundation. A relational perspective will have us remember that as "tools of communal dialogue," rights can be viewed as "a vocabulary used by community members to interpret and reinterpret their relationships with one another" (Minow, 1987, pp. 1890–1891).

Furthermore rights are not the only critical tool we can use to challenge abuses within relationships of unequal power. The ethics of care, we shall argue, can also serve this function. But first we must consider what the critics claim are obstacles to its doing so.

Are Justice and Care Enough?

Just as there are barriers with rights, some claim that there are also barriers we can encounter with a care perspective. One central worry is the ethics of care's alleged inability to focus on social structures, and its consequent limited scope of moral critique. Jaggar (1995) and others such as Card (1990) and Hoagland (1990) see care's attention to a situation's specificity and particularity as sometimes a "significant liability." For example, in cases of sexual harassment, focusing on particular female students and what they experience may well help us to see the effects insensitive and bullying behavior can have on them, but "it can also divert moral attention away from the social structures of privilege that legitimate such behavior" (Jaggar, 1995, p. 195).

Alison Jaggar considers both justice, which condemns sexual harassment as a violation of individual rights, as well as care, inadequate. Her point is that

> neither care nor justice reasoning as ordinarily construed constitute[s] the kind of hermeneutical moral thinking capable of questioning conventional definitions of assault as well as of exploring the complex assumptions about sexuality, aggression, and gender that make . . . [sexual harassment] not only thinkable but predictable and even normal. (p. 198)

Because we have observed the powerful normalizing role of social conventions, we concur with Jaggar's insistence on the need to keep a focus on structural problems, but we are less pessimistic than she about the ethics of care and justice, for we see elements in both that can help.

One of these elements is the publicity criterion in contractarian theories of justice. For example, John Rawls (1971) contends that contractarian theories of justice must establish *public* systems of rules such that "everyone engaged in it knows what he [or she] would know if these rules and his [or her] participation in the activity they define were the result of an agreement" (p. 56). And it is clear that "A person taking part in a [just] institution knows what the rules demand of him [or her] and of others.

He [or she] also knows that the others know this and that they know that he [or she] knows this" (p. 56).

We can note that the spirit of justice, on Rawls's conception, would seem to support the idea that persons should not be subject to rules about sexual harassment without knowing "what [they] would know if these rules and [their] participation in the activity they define were the result of an agreement." Not surprisingly, Kurt Baier (1958), whom Rawls follows on this point, calls his condition of publicity the "teachability" criterion. Attempting to design school sexual harassment policies so as to meet an approximate version of Rawls's publicity condition or Baier's teachability criterion leads us to ask: what would students need to know if these rules and their participation in these sexual harassment policies were to be Rawls's "result of an agreement"? This is one of the central questions we would take from a justice perspective to put at the forefront in shaping school sexual harassment policies.

The ethics of care also has its own educational answer to the worry critics raise about how to reveal and resist the entrenched power of structural inequalities. The answer, briefly stated, is to give primacy to moral education. The task, as Noddings (1996) says, "is to study, both philosophically and empirically, why we harm or refuse to harm one another and why we care or refuse to care for one another as we satisfy our deeply felt desire to belong" (p. 266).

Jane Roland Martin (1992), another proponent of revising education so as to emphasize the three Cs of care, concern, and connection, answers Jaggar's worry more directly. Martin argues that we need to introduce a gender-sensitive approach to studying care which makes the questionable social patterns of behavior an object of explicit study.

Student-to-student sexual harassment, as we have noted, occurs as part of a pattern in which students are caught in social circumstances that they themselves need to understand. It makes sense, therefore, to bring students into the conversation. In her book *The Schoolhome* (1992), Martin gives us some clear examples. In one imagined classroom she depicts a girl and boy having just performed the scene about the sun and moon from Act IV of Shakespeare's *The Taming of the Shrew* in which Petruchio insists that Kate say the sun is the moon.

> The teacher asks them why Petruchio forces Kate to say what is patently untrue. One of the onlookers in the class mutters, "No problem. He's a practical joker." But the boy who is going to play Petruchio in another scene of the play says, "I am not. I'm trying to get her to obey me." "You're right," one of the girls interjects. "Petruchio says, I will be master of my own. She is my goods, my chattels," the students recite in unison. Then the teacher asks,

"What happens to people if you are constantly telling them that what they see isn't really there?" "They think they are crazy," a girls says; "My father does it to my mother all the time." "When this happens to someone," the teacher asks, "can she speak her mind?" "She doesn't even know her mind," the girl answers. (p. 114)

Martin then points out that "The ensuing silence has more meaning for the students than any words [might have]" (p. 114).

The students discuss how to do the final scene with Kate's long submission speech. Will they do it straight, or with irony?

They have a long conversation about how Kate's submission, whether genuine or not, is achieved. Is Petruchio by any chance brainwashing Kate? They discuss what effects male dominance has on the two parties. Does he drive her crazy or simply underground, turning her into a wily manipulator? Is he a joker or is he practicing a form of domestic battery? They ask what gives him the right to call her his goods, his chattels. Before her marriage was she her own person or her father's? And whose person is Petruchio? (pp. 114–115)

Martin notes that

In [the] safe atmosphere where students can talk about the domestic violence in the play's action and the misogyny in its language, sense Petruchio's sadism and Kate's pain, *Taming* . . . [is] an especially effective educational vehicle. . . . Like other Shakespeare plays it illuminates some of those big questions that all of us must confront. Its special virtue is that it raises questions that girls and boys in our culture face here and now: . . . What happens to women who speak out? . . . Can boys and girls, men and women live and work together without the one sex being dominant and the other submissive? (pp. 115–116)

The ethics of care's revisioning of education includes just such dialogue.

CONCLUSION

We cannot hope to develop effective school sexual harassment policies without making them the subject matter of educational study, which in turn entails acknowledging, discussing, and ultimately challenging the norms that support sexual harassment. Sexual equality needs to be enacted so that the norms, beliefs, values, and practices of equality are embodied throughout the entire school culture. In short, the policy is *performed*, not merely articulated. We have argued that the values of both care and justice are required to underwrite such educative revisions. Students, teachers, and staff can then develop the skills, knowledge, and discernment needed to act in accord with existing legal policies, but more important, they can cultivate relationships in which such policies would in large measure become superfluous.

REFERENCES

American Association of University Women Educational Forum. (1993). *Hostile hallways: The AAUW survey on sexual harassment in America's schools.* Washington, DC: Nan Stein.
Baier, Kurt. (1958). *The moral point of view.* Ithaca, NY: Cornell University Press.
Card, Claudia. (1990). Caring and evil. *Hypatia, 5*(1), 101–108.
Eder, Donna. (1995). *School talk: Gender and Adolescent culture.* New Brunswick, NJ: Rutgers University Press.
Fine, Michelle, (Ed.). (1992). *Disruptive voices: The possibilities of feminist research.* Ann Arbor: University of Michigan Press.
Fine, Michelle. (1993). Sexuality, schooling, and adolescent females: The missing discourse of desire. In Lois Weiss & Michelle Fine (Eds.), *Beyond silenced voices: Class, race, and gender in United States schools* (pp. 75–100). Albany: State University of New York Press.
Fine, Michelle, & Macpherson, Pat. (1992). Over dinner: Femininism and adolescent female bodies. In Michelle Fine (Ed.), *Disruptive voices: The possibilities of feminist research.* (pp. 175–204). Ann Arbor: University of Michigan Press.
Frye, Marilyn. (1983). *The politics of reality.* Trumansburg, NY: Crossing Press.
Gilligan, Carol. (1982). *In a different voice.* Cambridge, MA: Harvard University Press.
Gilligan, Carol, Lyons, Nona, & Hammer, Trudy (Eds.). (1990). *Women, girls and psychotherapy: Reframing resistance.* New York: Harrington Park Press.
Hoagland, Sarah. (1990). Some concerns about Nel Noddings' caring. *Hypatia, 5*(1), 109–114.
Jaggar, Alison. (1995). Caring as a feminist practice of moral reason. In Virginia Held (Ed.), *Justice and care: Essential readings in feminist ethics* (pp. 179–202). Boulder: Westview Press.
Knopp, Fay. (1991). Community solutions to sexual violence. In Harold Pepinsky & Richard Quinney (Eds.), *Criminology as peace making* (pp. 183–192). Bloomington: Indiana University Press.
Larkin, June. (1994). *Sexual harassment: High school girls speak out.* Toronto: Second Story Press.
Lewis, John, & Hastings, Susan. (1994). *Sexual harassment in education.* Topeka, KS: National Organization on Legal Problems in Education.
MacKinnon, Catharine. (1979). *Sexual harassment of working women.* New Haven: Yale University Press.
MacKinnon, Catharine. (1987). *Feminism unmodified: Discourses on life and law.* Cambridge, MA: Harvard University Press.

Mann, Judith. (1994). *The difference: Discovering the hidden ways we silence girls: Finding alternatives that can give them a voice*. New York: Warner Books.

Martin, Jane Roland. (1992). *The schoolhome: Rethinking schools for changing families*. Cambridge, MA: Harvard University Press.

Minow, Martha. (1987). Interpreting rights: An essay for Robert Cover. *The Yale Law Journal, 96*(8),1860–1915.

Minow, Martha. (1990). *Making all the difference: Inclusion, exclusion, and American law*. Ithaca, NY: Cornell University Press.

Noddings, Nel. (1984). *Caring: A feminine approach to ethics and moral education*. Berkeley: University of California Press.

Noddings, Nel. (1987). Do we really want to produce good people? *Journal of Moral Education, 16*(3), 177–188.

Noddings, Nel. (1990). Ethics from the standpoint of women. In Deborah Rhode (Ed.), *Theoretical perspectives on sexual difference* (pp. 160–173). New Haven, CT: Yale University Press.

Noddings, Nel. (1992). *The challenge to care in schools: An alternative approach to education*. New York: Teachers College Press.

Noddings, Nel. (1996). On community. *Educational Theory, 46*(3), 245–267.

Orenstein, Peggy. (1994). *Schoolgirls: Young women, self-esteem, and the confidence gap*. New York: Doubleday.

Oyster River Cooperative School District Sexual Harassment and Policy Guidelines. April, 1994.

Pipher, Mary. (1994). *Reviving Ophelia: Saving the lives of adolescent girls*. New York: Ballantine Books.

Rawls, John. (1971). *A theory of justice*. Cambridge, MA: Harvard University Press.

Rich, Adrienne. (1979). *On lies, secrets, and silence: Selected prose, 1966–1978*. New York: Norton.

Ruddick, Sara. (1995). Injustice in families: Assault and domination In Virginia Held (Ed.), *Justice and care: Essential readings in feminist ethics* (pp. 203–223).Boulder: Westview Press.

Sherer, M. L. (1994). No longer just child's play: School liability under Title IX for peer sexual harassment. *University of Pennsylvania Law Review, 141*, 2119–2168.

Shoop, Robert, & Edwards, Debra. (1994). *How to stop sexual harassment in our schools: A handbook and curriculum guide for administrators and teachers*. Boston, MA: Allyn and Bacon.

Stein, Nan. (1993). It happens here, too: Sexual harassment and child sexual abuse in elementary and secondary schools. In S. K. Pollard & D. Pollard (Eds.), *Gender and Education* (pp. 191–203). Chicago: University of Chicago Press.

Stein, Nan. (1995, June). Is it sexually charged, sexually hostile, or the constitution?: Sexual harassment in K–12 schools. *Education Law Reporter, 98*, 621–631.

Stein, Nan, & Sjostrom, Lisa. (1994). *Flirting or hurting?: A teacher's guide on student to student sexual harassment in schools*. Washington, DC: National Education Association.

Strauss, Joanne. (1993). Peer sexual harassment of high school students: A reasonable student standard and an affirmative duty imposed on educational institutions. *Law and Inequality, 10,* 163–186.

Strauss, Susan. (1992). *Sexual harassment and teens.* Minneapolis, MN: Free Spirit.

Streitmatter, Jean. (1994). *Toward Gender equity in the classroom: Everyday teachers' beliefs and practices.* Albany: State University of New York Press.

Thorne, Barrie. (1994). *Gender play: Girls and boys in school.* New Brunswick, NJ: Rutgers University Press.

Wendell, Susan. (1990). Oppression and victimization; choice and responsibility. *Hypatia, 5*(3), 15–43.

Three Pictures
of Justice and Caring

Kenneth A. Strike

In Plato's *Crito* (1928), Crito objects to Socrates' decision not to flee the death penalty rendered against him by the Athenian court. He tells Socrates:

> I should say that you were betraying your children; for you might bring them up and educate them; instead of which you go away and leave them, and they will have to take their chances; and if they do not meet with the usual fate of orphans, there will be no thanks to you. No man should bring children into the world who is unwilling to persevere to the end in their nurture and education. (p. 144)

Socrates responds by taking the part of the laws of Athens who say to him:

> in your present attempt you are going to do us wrong. For after having brought you into the world, and nurtured and educated you, and given you every good that we had to give, we further proclaim and give the right to every Athenian, that if he does not like us when he has come of age . . . he may go where he pleases and take his goods with him. . . . And he who dis-

obeys us is . . . thrice wrong; first, because in disobeying us he is disobeying his parents; secondly, because we are the authors of his education; thirdly, because he has made an agreement with us that he will duly obey our commands. (p. 153)

There is much in these passages that suggests the picture of justice that feminist scholars have critiqued. Socrates is asked to avoid death in order to care for his children. This appeal to care is responded to by an argument in which the welfare of his children disappears as a consideration, in which a concern for civic life trumps a concern for family life, and in which a contract with the laws, an appeal to consistency, trumps the need to nurture one's children. Even though education and nurturance are mentioned, they are ascribed to an abstract agent, the laws, which is substituted for the family. And Plato does not help us to see these events from the perspective of Socrates' children or his wife, Xanthippe, whom he has made the prototype of a shrew.

When justice wears this face, the essential direction of the feminist critique has considerable force, and we owe the scholars who have developed it a debt for reminding us that human life is not lived exclusively in the public sphere and that no view which excludes relationships, family, nurturance, or children can be adequate. When justice is constructed so as to shoulder these values aside, it is more vice than virtue.

Consider, however, another picture. Martin Luther King's (1986) "I Have a Dream" speech contains these passages:

One hundred years later, the life of the Negro is still sadly crippled by the manacles of segregation and the chains of discrimination. One hundred years later, the Negro lives on a lonely island of poverty in the midst of a vast ocean of material prosperity. One hundred years later, the Negro is still languishing in the corners of American society and finds himself an exile in his own land. I have a dream that one day the state of Alabama, whose governor's lips are presently dripping with the words of interposition and nullification, will be transformed into a situation where little black boys and black girls will be able to join hands with little white boys and white girls and walk together as sisters and brothers. . . . This is our hope. This is the faith with which I return to the South. With this faith we will be able to hew out of the mountain of despair a stone of hope. With this faith we will be able to transform the jangling discords of our nation into a beautiful symphony of brotherhood. With this faith we will be able to work together, to pray together, to struggle together, to go to jail together, to stand up for freedom together, knowing that we will be free one day. (p. 219)

Note three things about King's "I Have a Dream" speech. First, it appeals to some of the same considerations to which Socrates appeals. There is an appeal to consistency. Americans are asked to live up to what they have said in the *Declaration of Independence* and the Fourteenth Amendment. There is an appeal to justice and equality. There are, however, two differences. First, King notes the consequences of inequality for the welfare of African Americans, how they are isolated and impoverished by it. Second, King paints a picture of a just community which is far more than a place where rules are followed with impartiality. It is one in which blacks and whites are friends, comrades, brothers, and sisters. Here the opposition between justice and care seems largely dissolved. Justice is the enemy of poverty and alienation, and the friend of community, solidarity, and relationship. Justice is caring's handmaiden and compatriot. King's picture of justice is a poorer target for the feminist critique than that of Socrates. Indeed, it seems to picture justice in a way that appeals to the core values of caring and nurturance.

Consider a third picture. Americans have recently noted the passage of the fortieth anniversary of the integration of Little Rock High School. I was in my early teens when this occurred. I remember it vividly if not in detail. There were several black children who were taken to school by U. S. federal marshals. The governor of Arkansas, Orville Faubus, made a show of resistance, but yielded to superior federal power. What I remember most clearly was the mob of white people spewing hatred at frightened black children. I have never forgotten it. It frightened me. I could see myself as one of those children. I did not understand it. What had they done? How could anyone hate children? Couldn't the mob see their fear? Why didn't they stop? Why did these children want to go to that school where they were so unwelcome? What would it be like to stay there once the marshals were gone? This was beyond my experience. I had no answers to these questions.

I have come to understand the legal context of this event quite well. I have written on desegregation, and I teach the case law on it on a regular basis. I have come to appreciate the difficulties and complexities associated with it and to feel frustration at how it has worked out. But I still find the hatred of that crowd frightening and incomprehensible.

I have other questions now. I can put myself in the place of the parents of these children more easily now that I have been a parent. I wonder, if I would have put my children in such a situation. I think, perhaps, that these parents were courageous. I wonder, though, if they did what they did because they cared for their children, or because they cared for their cause. Perhaps both. I also wonder if their care for their children was an obstacle. I know that had I been asked to put my children in harm's way, I would have found it hard. I would have wondered if I was sacrificing them to a cause that was mine more than theirs. I would have worried that I was doing real harm to them for the sake of an abstraction. Even if I had discussed the matter carefully with them and they had seemed to understand and to agree, I would have wondered if I had manipulated them or if I should not have stopped them. I worry about my own children that way. My daughter, recently graduated as an environmental engineer, wants to join an international relief agency, go to a third world country, and to do what she can to help make other people's lives better. I am very proud of that desire in her. But a voice within, neither still nor small, says, "Please don't. Stay home. Be safe."

I imagine the parents of these Little Rock children had similar thoughts and faced a similar dilemma. I am glad that these parents and their children did this. For one, their courage made me, in some small way, a better person. I suspect there are many others for whom this is true. And I do not see these parents as dismissing the care that they had for their children as an irrelevance, but as struggling with it and counting the threat to their children as a high cost. Here too there is a picture of justice and caring. Perhaps it has something in common with both that of Socrates and of Martin Luther King. Here family is set aside for a while in order for one to pursue justice in the civic arena. At the same time the values of family, nurturance, and caring are not dismissed. I imagine these parents showed their children their care and love through these struggles. While they risked the welfare of their children, I imagine they also sought better lives for them and for other black children. This element of struggle is something this picture has in common with that of Dr. King's. The "I Have a Dream" speech also takes note of the costs.

However, I think that this third picture emphasizes something the others do not. It focuses attention on the conflict between justice and caring and the need to make hard choices. It adds moral complexity and the need to balance conflicting moral goods. The cost of struggle here is not abstract. These parents could not think about it in any moral cost benefit analysis that abstractly weighs the social gains against the human costs. For these parents, these are not just *some* children; these are *our* children. So any balance to be struck is not to be thought of just as a social abstraction, but as having real and potentially disastrous effects on particular loved ones. In this case, in a sense, parents must weigh and balance justice and caring, but they cannot let go of either.

Think of these three examples as candidates for paradigm cases of how the relationship between justice and caring might be pictured. (And I want to note that they are more of an attempt to paint pictures than to develop detailed analytic categories.) How do they help? Here I want to make three suggestions.

First, I think the picture people hold of the paradigm case of the relationship between justice and caring may be more important to their views than some of the issues of technical philosophy that distinguish various authors in this book. Second, I think that the first and the third pictures have tended to dominate much of what has been written about justice and caring. To a degree that continues here. While there are the beginnings of inquiries into approaches that see justice and caring as complementary, that the issue is *justice versus caring* is still central to many of the articles in this volume. Finally, I think more attention should be given to developing the second picture, and that doing so may be the crucial matter in thinking about education and schooling.

Almost all of the authors in this volume agree on some things. No one is against justice or caring. The authors who have been most critical of justice nevertheless here grant it a place in the moral life. Those who have talked much about justice throughout their professional lives, and certainly I would count myself a chief among such sinners, have no wish to defend what I have represented as the Socratic stance. Both justice and caring count. And they count in all areas of life.

However, a number of authors focus on the ways in which justice and caring are in tension. There are different philosophical accounts of this tension. Some authors may be more inclined to see such tension as exists between justice and caring as the expression of two different moral stances or forms of moral reasoning. Others seem to see the difference as one between different moral goods. Still others have noted that most people employ both kinds of notions in their moral discourse and that sometimes the vocabularies of justice and caring seem to blend and be translatable.

Perhaps, however, these technical philosophical issues are not all or even the most important thing that is going on. It may be that the picture we have of the paradigm case of the relationship between justice and caring is the more crucial factor in the stance taken. I suspect that for some authors in this volume, the first picture is the one that dominates. Justice is seen as too often shouldering care aside, as treating it as an irrelevance, of preferring civic life to family life and personal relationships. When this happens, they argue, justice is more vice than virtue. When justice shoulders caring aside, there is potential for harm. In education, real children may be unnecessarily turned into a means of pursuing moral abstractions. While these authors may not reject justice, what they seek is a restoration of caring in human life as well as in philosophical accounts.

Is this first picture of justice valid? Surely it is. Whether or not it is the dominant picture of justice in the Western philosophical tradition I do not profess to know, but it is surely there. And there are surely cases in current educational policy where justice seems to shoulder caring aside. When it does, the protest against it seems well targeted and the concern to restore a role for caring important.

Other articles in the book seem more moved by the third picture. They do not see justice as excluding caring, but they do tend to see justice and caring as competitive. They tend to want to affirm both commitments while acknowledging that they may be in tension. Thus they are likely to be impressed by the need to strike a balance and by the need to reveal moral complexity and ambiguity.

What can be said for the second picture? Let me describe another variation of it. I shall emphasize some of the religious traditions on which Martin Luther King drew. Consider one emphasis in the prophetic tradition found in the Old Testament. The prophet Micah writes:

> Will the Lord be pleased with thousands of rams, or with ten thousands of rivers of oil? Shall I give my firstborn for my transgression, the fruit of my body for the sin of my soul? He hath shewed thee, O man, what is good; and what doth the Lord require of thee, but to do justly, and to love mercy, and to walk humbly with thy God? (Micah 6:7-8)

The context of this passage is a protest by the prophet against the exploitation of the poor and the corruption of justice by a religious and political elite, an elite that was scrupulous in following the ordinances of the law. It says that God is not moved by adherence to religious law when those who follow the law also oppress the poor. God expects justice, mercy, and humility. God is on the side of the poor. Here is a picture of justice in which justice and caring work together and are in harmony. Justice is not associated with the following of rules come what may. Indeed, it is carefully distinguished from a certain kind of rule following.

In this vision, justice is also associated with notions such as forgiveness and reconciliation. It focuses on the restoration of relationships when they are broken by injustice and oppression. It is, perhaps, better realized by South Africa's Court of Truth and Reconciliation or by the Navajo peacemaking process[1] than by the procedures of the American judicial system. Justice is for the sake of a form of community, one in which the poor are not oppressed, one in which all can live decent lives, one in which solidarity and mutual concern dominate, one in which reconciliation and forgiveness are more important goals than retribution. The distinctiveness and power of Martin Luther King's pleas for justice, I think, consist in wedding this strain in our religious tradition with the civic ideals of America. It is why a society that lives up to the *Declaration of Independence* and the Fourteenth Amendment is one where "little black boys and black girls will be able to join hands with little white boys and white girls and

---

1. See Witmer (1996). I owe the examples in this paragraph to David Harris.

walk together as sisters and brothers." I do not think it a stretch here to suggest that in this vision, justice is seen as being in the service of community, relationship, nurturance, and caring.

I do not see this picture as a grand theory of society or as an all-encompassing picture of the moral life of the sort that those of us who argue for moral pluralism seek to resist. It is not so much a unified philosophical theory as a vision in which we carefully attend to all that is important and work to find ways in which our ideals can serve one another.

Is one of these three pictures the right picture? We need to be careful how we understand this question. We might mean, "Does one of these pictures characterize how justice and care really are in the world?" Or we might mean, "To which of these pictures should we aspire?" In the first case, I suspect that the best answer is that we should be careful not to overgeneralize any one picture. I suspect that we can find real cases of each, although perhaps cases which actually exemplify justice and caring working in a symbiotic way are depressingly few.

To what should we aspire? Perhaps we should give more credence to a vision such as that of Martin Luther King. That is, perhaps we should emphasize a view of justice that does not take as its central point a formal notion of impartial treatment, but that seeks to help everyone lead good lives as they conceive them in harmony with others. Perhaps. But what I have just said is notoriously vague. Any attempt to cash it out will quickly confront the many difficulties and ambiguities associated with the notion of community and communitarian thought generally.

I will have a few thoughts on this in a moment. First, however, I think there is much about American education which suggests that the first picture is still very much with us. Consider that much of the educational-policy-making community is now engaged in a debate that might be characterized as a state-versus-market debate. On the state side is a view of reform, often described as systemic reform, that believes that public schools can be reformed through standards and accountability systems. On the other is a group who argues that public monopolies are inherently inefficient and claims that schools need the discipline of Adam Smith's invisible hand. Most of the participants in this debate share some things. They are dominated by a concern for international competitiveness and human capital formation, and they are focused on raising academic achievement as measured by standardized tests.

While a concern for justice is not central in this debate, justice occasionally makes a cameo appearance. There are discussions of equity in funding and worries about stratification and the failure of urban school systems. It is, however, an argument mostly about measured gains in achievement, an argument waged by economists armed with regression equations. One thing that seems absent from these debates is a concern for caring or nurturance. Another is a concern for the shape of school communities.

Here it may be useful to look at an example of schools where these concerns are not absent. In their book *Catholic Schools and the Common Good*, Bryk, Lee, and Holland (1993) claim that Catholic schools share three characteristics: a commitment to academic success for all students, a sense of the school as a caring environment, and an inspirational ideology. They have a vision that emphasizes shaping persons in community, predicated on a belief in the dignity of each human being and in the responsibility of each to advance peace, justice, and human welfare. Bryk et al. claim that Catholic schools have evolved away from being narrowly sectarian institutions and that they now provide an alternative to public schools which are dominated by norms that are individualistic, competitive, and materialistic—norms which socialize students to accept inequality as inevitable and deserved. Indeed, they claim that Catholic schools are closer to the common school ideal than are public schools.

Note two things about this. First, this description of Catholic schools shares much of the vision of Martin Luther King. The languages of justice and caring are woven together. Both are there. Neither is neglected. Justice is for the sake of caring and human flourishing. Second, Catholic schools, while they are not dominated by a concern for academic achievement or by economic considerations, do well by their students in both cases.

There is, however, a small dark cloud on this horizon. Catholic schools may no longer be narrowly sectarian, but they are still Catholic. That they successfully educate many minority students who are not Catholic is praiseworthy. But it does not mean that Catholic schools are open to the expression of diverse forms of religiosity. One may not have to be a Catholic to be welcomed in a Catholic school, but this does not mean that one may easily express one's Jewishness or one's Presbyterianness there.

One should not expect Catholic schools to affirm a commitment to religious neutrality, but we do expect this of public schools. They cannot be sectarian. Thus a pressing question arises: How central is the humanistic tradition of Catholicism that since Vatican II has asserted its influence in Catholic schools to the kinds of caring, justice-seeking communities that Bryk et al. claim these schools often are? Can we have communities such as these without the Catholicism or apart from some other functionally equivalent view? Do we need the inspiration ideology?

This points to larger question. What is the basis of good, caring, nurturing, justice-seeking communities? From what do they draw their motivation? How are they created and sustained? What are they like? Is their ultimate source to be found in natural caring? In religious conviction? What kinds of institutions do they require? Do they require what many now refer to as "civil society" to sustain them? I don't know. But I think the justice/caring discussion leads us to these larger questions, to the quest for a more inclusive moral vision for school communities.

Consider that American schools are routinely beset by the thorny question of how we can be one while still being many. We cannot just affirm the worth of community. Communities are constituted in part by shared values. Which ones? Whose? When we constitute a community through shared values, we draw a circle. Some are inside, some are outside. That is not always a bad thing. The right of free association permits us to band together in particularistic communities to pursue common interests. There is no injustice when believers in a particular faith choose to meet together and to exclude those who do not share it.

But values that include and exclude in this way cannot be the basis of school communities when those schools are public schools. What can? Here the dilemma has this character. A set of values sufficient to constitute a public school must be "thick" enough to bind people together in a just and caring community and to motivate an educational project. But these values must not be so thick so as to exclude some or to make some into second-class citizens.

Does Martin Luther King's vision provide a possible vision for public schools? Much in me wants to say that it can. But at the same time, we must note that it is rooted in a religious tradition which King uses as a lens to reinterpret central American ideas into a vision of community. This vision is not so thick as the Catholicism that forges Catholic schools, but its religious content may make it too thick still.

Here one has to ask whether the vision could be stated in a form that is thick enough to be community constituting and thin enough not to exclude or marginalize. We need also to ask whether such a vision can motivate an educational program. The vision that informs a Catholic school involves not only a commitment to caring and justice. It brings to educational decision making a humanistic theological tradition developed by Catholic thinkers from Aquinas to Maritan. This humanistic tradition helps to answer questions about such issues as the value of knowledge. It is not clear that there is anything in King's vision that does this kind of work. If not, then the values that constitute a school community may need to be thicker than the values that constitute King's vision.

Might caring be enough to constitute school communities? We might say that if there is caring, then people can be bound together in stable and nurturing communities in which the diversity of their individual educational views of the good and their individual educational projects is respected and nurtured. And I think this is a tempting thing to say as well. But I am doubtful. To consider why, suppose we distinguish two elements in care. One element is the idea that nurturance is essential to human growth and development. A second is that relationships are an important part of any reasonable conception of a good life.

I assume these two claims to be true. What questions do they pose when we ask about schools? When we look at nurturance in the context of public schooling, we are likely to want to say things like this: nurturance is essential if children are to grow up to be healthy and decent people; nurturance is essential if they are to learn. Thus we should see to it that all children are educated in schools where nurturance is provided. These claims point us back to the critique of much of educational policy. If they are true, why does nurturance seem absent from so much educational discussion?

Also, however, when we ask how all children can be nurtured, we begin to treat nurturance as a distributable commodity and to raise questions of justice. If every child should have it, then if some children do and some don't, that is unfair. How can we rectify this injustice? What policies do we need to be sure that every child is nurtured? How can we have communities in which every child is cared for? I doubt that an ethic of caring can move from the realm of personal relationships into the realm of educational policy without generating its own questions of distributive justice. Insofar as this is true, caring cannot stand alone as the basis of school communities.

Relationships are a good. I hope almost everyone will agree. But I doubt that relationships are the only good or the supreme good. And I don't think those whose views emphasize caring have claimed this. There are other goods. If so, we need ways to think about what they are. If we care for others, one thing we will do is to respect their sense of what is good and to respect the diversity of educational projects that flow from these sources. But this does not excuse us from the need to provide students resources to think about their own view of a good life and a good education.

These resources may be of diverse sorts. There may be conversational forums where such issues are raised and discussed. These will surely include some exploration of religious, philosophical, and cultural sources. What kinds of institutions are required? Will we want schools where there is a marketplace of ideas and a conversation between traditions? Will we want schools in which one tradition reigns and is more deeply explored? Is there some middle ground here? I don't propose to answer any such questions. My point is that as a view of caring tries to address complex and contentious issues of schooling, it will find it hard to avoid such questions. It will find that it has a piece of a vision of human flourishing, but that there are other pieces. It will find that it has to address the question of how relationships fit into a larger package of educational goods. It will find it has raised questions of justice of its own. It will probably have to step outside of an understanding of caring to address these kinds of questions. It will need more than caring to constitute community.

Perhaps, however, the most important thing to say here is that in asking these questions it is especially important that we not allow justice to shoulder caring aside. When we do so, we take a step toward the culture wars in which incommensurable views about how we are entitled to be treated in schools and about whose views should triumph become central. If we are to seek mutually satisfactory solutions to these difficult questions, we will need to address one another in a spirit of caring and mutual concern. Caring may not be a sufficient base for conceptualizing what counts as a good educational community, but it surely is required by the attempt to achieve one.

Now I will briefly return to the three pictures of the relationship between justice and caring. It is useful and important to say that when justice shoulders aside caring, it is more vice than virtue. It is useful to say that sometimes moral goods conflict and that we need the wisdom to balance them. But when we pose the issues of justice and caring in the context of the question "What kinds of communities should schools be?" we need to begin the work of developing a vision such as that of Martin Luther King. We need to ask how justice and caring hang together in a praiseworthy view of schooling.

I am hopeful the essays in this volume will be seen as moving us toward achieving this larger task. To be sure, they present conflicting views about some of the tensions between justice and caring. However, they also begin the hard work of connecting these questions to the questions of policy, pedagogy, and practice that need to be answered to construct good school communities, and they begin to attach the justice and caring debate to a larger range of questions. When a group of authors from quite different traditions on these issues are able to say "Justice and caring both count," when they can ask "How can we keep justice from shouldering aside caring and nurturance? How can we find the wisdom to balance them when they are in tension? And how can we find ways to make them work together in a way that furthers human flourishing?" that is a helpful beginning.

REFERENCES

Bryk, Anthony S., Lee, Valerie E., & Holland, Peter, B. (1993). *Catholic schools and the common good*. Cambridge, MA: Harvard University Press.

King, Martin Luther. (1986). I have a dream. In James Melvin Washington (Ed.), *A testimony of hope: The essential writings of Martin Luther King* (pp. 215-219). San Francisco: Harper & Row.

Plato. (1928). Crito. In Benjamin Jowett (Ed.), *Works of Plato* (Vol. 3; pp. 135-158). New York: Tudor.

Witmer, Sharon. (1996, Summer). Making peace, the Navajo way. *Tribal College Journal, 8*(1), 24-26.

About the Editors and Contributors

William L. Blizek is Professor of Philosophy and Religion at the University of Nebraska at Omaha, where he teaches courses on ethics, social philosophy, human values in medicine, self-deception, and religion and film. He is particularly interested in ethical issues in literature and film. Dr. Blizek has published or read a number of papers on issues of caring, including "Ethics and the Educational Community," "Caring in the Classroom," "Ethical Caring," and "If Caring Were King." He also is the co-editor of *The Journal of Religion and Film*.

Lawrence Blum is Professor of Philosophy and Distinguished Professor of Liberal Arts and Education at the University of Massachusetts at Boston. He has also taught at the Stanford School of Education and Teachers College, Columbia University. His Ph.D. in philosophy is from Harvard University. He is the author of *Friendship, Altruism, and Morality* (1980) and *Moral Perception and Particularity* (1994) and many articles on ethics, moral development, race, and multicultural education, including "Multicultural Education as Values Education" (1997). He has received two fellowships from the National Endowment for the Humanities.

Elizabeth Chamberlain brings twenty-five years of experience and multiple perspectives to the issue of justice and care in education. She has been a classroom teacher, special education teacher, guidance counselor, and administrator in middle-level education, and has been instrumental in the design and implementation of sexual harassment policies in schools. She received her doctorate in education from the University of New Hampshire in 1997 and has taught in teacher preparation programs at the University of New Hampshire, Durham, New Hampshire, and Dominican University in River Forest, Illinois. She is currently assistant professor of education at Franklin Pierce College in Rindge, New Hampshire, where she continues her research on gender equity issues in education.

Ann Diller is a professor and Director of Doctoral Studies in Education at the University of New Hampshire. She holds the UNH Lindberg Award for Outstanding Teacher-Scholar. She was the 1998 president of the Philosophy of Education Society. Recent publications include her co-authored book, *The Gender Question in Education: Theory, Pedagogy, and Politics* (Westview Press, 1996), an essay entitled "In Praise of Objective-

Subjectivity: Teaching the Pursuit of Precision" (*Studies in Philosophy and Education, 16*), and her PES presidential address, "Facing the Torpedo Fish: Becoming a Philosopher of One's Own Education."

Barbara Houston is Class of 1944 Professor of Education at the University of New Hampshire. Her previous teaching at the University of Western Ontario won an award from the Ontario Confederation of University Faculty Associations. Her research work is in feminist theory, ethics, and philosophy of education. She is co-author of *The Gender Question in Education: Theory, Pedagogy, and Politics* (Westview Press, 1996). Her current research interests are in the area of moral psychology.

Michael S. Katz is a Professor of Education at San Jose State University; he has also taught at The American University and the University of Nebraska at Omaha; his primary research interest recently has been ethical issues in education. Michael Katz received his bachelor's degree from Amherst College and a master's and doctorate from Stanford University. He has been an active member of the Philosophy of Education Society for the past 25 years, having served as its Secretary-Treasurer and Chair of its Commission on Professional Affairs. His articles have appeared in *Educational Theory, The Journal of Teacher Education, Interchange, The Journal of Learning Disabilities*, and *The Proceedings of the Philosophy of Education Society*.

Rita S. Manning is a Philosopher at San Jose State University. She specializes in ethics, feminism, and social and political philosophy. She is the author of *Speaking From the Heart* and co-editor (with Rene Trujillo) of *Social Justice in a Diverse Society*. She has authored over 20 articles on subjects ranging from Greek philosophy to medical ethics.

Nel Noddings is the Lee Jacks Professor of Education Emerita at Stanford University and Professor of Philosophy and Education at Teachers College, Columbia University. Her most recent book is *Caregiving* (co-edited with Suzanne Gordon and Patricia Benner).

Dawn E. Schrader is Associate Professor of Educational Psychology at Cornell University. She received her doctorate in Human Development and Psychology from Harvard University in 1988 under the direction of Lawrence Kohlberg (until 1987) and Robert Kegan. Her primary research interest is the exploration of the metacognitive processes underlying self-reflective thinking and how such processes relate to the actions and choices individuals make in their work and in their lives. She conducts research on the interaction between professors' and college students' moral, self, and epistemological development.

Kenneth A. Strike is Professor of Philosophy of Education at Cornell University. He is the author of *The Ethics of Teaching, The Ethics of School Administration*, and numerous other books and articles. He is past president of the Philosophy of Education Society and is a member of the National Academy of Education.

Index